D1555960

WAFFEN-SS UNIFORMS & INSIGNIA

WAFFEN-⚡⚡ UNIFORMS & INSIGNIA

Wade Krawczyk & Peter v Lukacs

The Crowood Press

First published in 2001 by
The Crowood Press Ltd
Ramsbury, Marlborough
Wiltshire SN8 2HR

British Library Cataloguing-in-Publication Data
A catalogue record for this book is available
from the British Library

ISBN 1 86126 461 5

Edited by Martin Windrow
Designed by Frank Ainscough/Compendium
Printed and bound by Craft Print International Ltd

Acknowledgements:
As with any undertaking of this size, the authors cannot take
sole credit for all the hard work. Many individuals have given
their time, their support, and access to items from their collec-
tions during the preparation of this work. Our thanks go to:
William Angus, Petrus Bolin, Mike Cessford, Dave Doyle,
Blake Edgerton, Jeff Hopkins, Bart Jansen, Göran Landelius,
Niklas Ljusford, John Mihailov, Miklagaards Collectibles,
Peter Walter, and Dimitri Zatsepilov.
    Finally, Peter would like to express his thanks to his wife
Cilla, as well as to Stefan and Mikaila. Wade would like to
thank his wife Melissa, and his good friends for all the support
over the long term of this project. This book belongs to all of
you as well.   *WK & PL*

CONTENTS

Introduction 6
The Waffen-SS Divisions - SS Waffenfarbe - Waffen-SS ranks.

Headgear 10
General officers' service caps - officers' service caps - officers' 'old model' field cap -
NCOs' M1938 field cap - enlisted mens'/NCOs' service caps - officers' 'new model' field
cap - enlisted mens'/NCOs' 'new model' field cap - officers' mountain cap - officers' M1943
field cap - enlisted mens'/NCOs' M1943 field caps - steel helmets - camouflage helmet covers.

Service Uniforms 38
General officer's service tunic - officer's service uniform - officers' service tunics - enlisted
mens'/NCOs' service tunics M1936, M1940, M1944 - trousers M1944 - special tunic
for assault artillery.

Camouflage Uniforms 86
Camouflage smocks M1940, M1942 - camouflage tunic and trousers M1944 -
camouflage winter parka - camouflage winter trousers, gloves, hood - camouflage
Panzer tunics - camouflage Panzer trousers.

Waffen-SS Insignia 102
Collar patches, German and foreign volunteer - shoulder straps - shoulder strap devices -
sleeve eagles - cloth cap insignia - foreign volunteer arm shields - metal cap insignia - cuff titles.

Miscellanea 120
Mountain guides' badges - RZM labels - buttons - officers' belt and buckle - enlisted
ranks' belt and buckles - identity tags - awards and decorations - paybooks.

Select Bibliography 128

(Right) An SS-Rotten-führer (equivalent to a lance-corporal) wearing the Army-style M1940 tunic with a 'typical' set of insignia - i.e., slightly difficult to interpret. The cuff title with skull and crossbones ('death's-head') emblem of September 1938 pattern suggests a former member of Totenkopf-Standarte 1 'Oberbayern' now serving with the SS-Totenkopf-Division, probably before the order of September 1942 substituting a script 'Totenkopf' title for the emblem. He wears on his right collar the SS-runes rather than the death's-head authorised for most of the division. Within the division runes were authorised in March 1941 for

SS-T (Inf) Regt 9 (later renumbered 5) 'Thule', but the 'Thule' cuff title did not appear until at least mid-1942, which may place him in that unit between those dates.

The rank insignia on his left collar patch, the sleeve eagle and rank chevrons on his left sleeve, and the white piping of the black shoulderstraps are all conventional. The medal ribbons are those for the Iron Cross 2nd Class and Winter 1941/42 Eastern Front medal.

(Right) The silver-grey Tresse braid around the field-grey collar and black shoulderstraps of this apparently M1940 tunic identifies one of the grades of Scharführer (sergeants). The Totenkopf collar patches are here worn on both sides, in horizontal and 'non-mirrored' form. The

service cap appears to be a standard enlisted ranks' Dienstmütze (Schirm-mütze) with the chin strap and buttons removed and worn in the style of the 'old pattern field cap' or 'crusher cap'.

INTRODUCTION

There are several areas of particular popularity in the field of the study and collecting of German uniforms of the Second World War. Elite units such as the Fallschirmjäger, the Panzertruppe and the Afrikakorps generate intense interest among historical researchers and collectors; but no branch of the armed forces of the Third Reich commands as much attention as the Waffen-SS.

Born from a paramilitary and political background, and at first scorned by the regular Army for that reason, the Waffen-SS grew from small beginnings to become the fourth armed service of the state, with a strength of many hundreds of thousands of men. Its combat record was initially unimpressive; but within three years it had proved itself an innovative and competent fighting force, and in 1944-45 it was a genuine elite, highly regarded by its peers and feared by its enemies.

The innovative nature of this organisation was reflected in the design and use of various items of clothing and insignia. The Waffen-SS was the world's first military organisation to wholeheartedly embrace the concept of camouflage clothing and to make it available as general issue at unit and formation level; this is now regarded as the norm by armies the world over, but sixty years ago it was a novelty. As a reflection of its non-military background the Waffen-SS also adopted a new system of rank titles, and new designs of insignia based partly upon Germanic and Nordic runic symbols. Its insignia became more varied and striking as the organisation expanded to include many non-German units.

The purpose of this work is to illustrate surviving articles of clothing and insignia and to describe and explain them in a clear, concise fashion. The opening up of the former Soviet Union over the past decade had made wholly new sources of rare original items accessible to resourceful collectors in the West. Most of the items illustrated in these pages have been acquired in Russia and the Baltic states, and are published here for the first time.

There are variations of detail between many issue items, and when studying these one has to keep an open mind. Soldiers of the day cared little about conforming to the exact regulation standards which collectors today hold in such high regard. A soldier's clothing was work-wear, to protect him from the elements and to allow him to carry out his tasks efficiently; his insignia were to identify him as far as was necessary within his unit and, on walking-out uniform, to show off his allegiance and distinctions to the best effect. The problems of supply, especially in the latter part of the war, meant that repair or adaptation were normal practice, as was the manufacture of some items outside the regular procurement system. There is ample photographic evidence that uniforms and combinations of insignia were often not 'by the book'. At its best, the SS-Bekleidungswerke manufactured just 20 per cent of Waffen-SS clothing requirements; the rest was provided by drawing upon Army stocks.

In consequence, most Waffen-SS tunics, for example, will be found in the so-called 'Army pattern'. These are often rejected by purists as being in some sense 'not truly SS'; the evidence shows this to be incorrect. Again, the date of official orders replacing some item of uniform with a new pattern may be clearly recorded; but that does not mean that the old pattern was abandoned immediately - quartermasters, and individual officers and men, were often reluctant to do so even when sufficient new stocks had reached the front. The regulations governing the minutiae of insignia of units and formations, and of whole branches of service, were quite often changed, sometimes successively after short intervals. These regulations often took many months to become generally observed in the distant front lines of the Eastern Front - if they ever were.Such variety in details adds to the interest of the researcher's task and the collector's hobby; and the authors hope that readers will find the range of items illustrated in these pages both interesting and informative.

Note that throughout this text, terms such as 'silver', 'gold', 'silk', etc should be taken to mean 'made from materials having the appearance of...' - e.g., the 'silver bullion' wire used for officers' insignia and appointments was in fact made from bright aluminium.

WAFFEN-SS DIVISIONS

This book is no place for even the briefest history of a huge and complex organisation. However, in order to place in context the units and formations mentioned in the captions accompanying the photographs in this book, a basic listing of the Waffen-SS divisions may be useful. Titles are given in their final form. The date indicates when an existing formation was raised to divisional status (DS) or a new formation was first raised (R). Many of these divisions were expanded to that status on the basis of pre-existing brigades.

A number of the higher-numbered divisions were expanded, assembled or raised 'on paper', but had no meaningful military existence in practice; some have been identified only through field post office documentation. Those whose titles include the prefix *Freiwilligen* ('Volunteer') were raised from foreigners regarded as having 'honorary Aryan' status; some of these were granted the double-lightning SS runes on the right hand collar patch, but others displayed alternative insignia. Those with the prefix *Waffen* were 'non-Aryan', and wore various other traditional or invented collar patch motifs.

Within divisions all regiments were identified by numbers, some of which were changed during the course of the war; but a minority were also named, and some of these were granted the privilege of wearing a regimental cuff title. Initially some senior regiments also displayed numbers added to the SS rune collar patch. Since these features may be found on uniforms, we include mention of these units under the relevant divisions; note that a few units were transferred, normally as the cadre for newly-raised divisions. Ordinal numbers and national designations are given in the German form.

1. SS-Panzer-Division 'Leibstandarte SS Adolf Hitler' (DS June 1941)

2. SS-Panzer-Division 'Das Reich' (DS October 1939) Regts 'Deutschland' ('SS 1'), 'Germania' ('SS 2'), 'Der Führer' ('SS 3'), 'Langemark'

3. SS-Panzer-Division 'Totenkopf' (DS October 1939) Regts 'Thule', 'Theodor Eicke', 'SS-Heimwehr Danzig'

4. SS-Polizei-Panzer-Grenadier-Division (R October 1939)

5. SS-Panzer-Division 'Wiking' (R December 1940) Regts 'Germania' ('SS 2'), 'Westland', 'Nordland'

6. SS-Gebirgs-Division 'Nord' (DS June 1941) Regts 'Reinhard Heydrich', 'Michael Gaißmair', Bn 'Norge'

7. SS-Freiwilligen-Gebirgs-Division 'Prinz Eugen' (R March 1942) Regt 'Artur Phleps'

8. SS-Kavallerie-Division 'Florian Geyer' (DS June 1942)

9. SS-Panzer-Division 'Hohenstaufen' (R January 1943)

10. SS-Panzer-Division 'Frundsberg' (R February 1943)

11. SS-Freiwilligen-Panzer-Grenadier-Division 'Nordland' (R March 1943) Regts 'Norge', 'Danmark', Bn 'Hermann von Salza'

12. SS-Panzer-Division 'Hitlerjugend' (R June 1943)

13. Waffen-Gebirgs-Division der SS 'Handschar' (kroatische Nr.1) (R March 1943)

14. Waffen-Grenadier-Division der SS (ukrainische Nr.1) (R August 1943)

15. Waffen-Grenadier-Division der SS (lettische Nr.1) (R February 1943)

16. SS-Panzer-Grenadier-Division 'Reichsführer-SS' (DS October 1943)

17. SS-Panzer-Grenadier-Division 'Götz von Berlichingen' (R October 1943)

18. SS-Freiwilligen-Panzer-Grenadier-Division 'Horst Wessel' (DS January 1944)

19. Waffen-Grenadier-Division der SS (lettisches Nr.2) (DS January 1944)

20. Waffen-Grenadier-Division der SS (estnische Nr.1) (DS January 1944)

21. Waffen-Gebirgs-Division der SS 'Skanderbeg' (albanische Nr.1) (R April 1944)

22. SS-Freiwilligen-Kavallerie-Division 'Maria Theresia' (R spring 1944)

23. Waffen-Gebirgs-Division der SS 'Kama' (kroatische Nr.2) (R June 1944, disbanded September 1944)

23. SS-Freiwilligen-Panzer-Grenadier-Division 'Nederland' (DS February 1945) Regts 'General Seyffardt', 'De Ruiter'

24. Waffen-Gebirgs-(Karstjäger-)Division der SS (DS July 1944; reduced to brigade, December 1944)

25. Waffen-Grenadier-Division der SS 'Hunyadi' (ungarische Nr.1) (R May 1944)

26. Waffen-Grenadier-Division der SS ('Hungaria' or 'Gömbös' ?) (ungarische Nr.2) (R March 1945)

27. SS-Freiwilligen-Grenadier-Division 'Langemarck' (flämische Nr.1 ?) (DS September 1944)

28. SS-Freiwilligen-Grenadier-Division 'Wallonien' (DS October 1944)

29. Waffen-Grenadier-Division der SS (russische Nr.1?) (DS August-September 1944 ?)

29. Waffen-Grenadier-Division der SS (italienische Nr.1) (DS April 1945)

30. Waffen-Grenadier-Division der SS (russische Nr.2, weissruthenische Nr.1 ?) (DS August 1944)

31. SS-Freiwilligen-Grenadier-Division ('Böhmen-Mähren' ?) (R October 1944)

32. SS-Freiwilligen-Grenadier-Division '30 Januar' (R January 1945)

33. Waffen-Kavallerie-Division der SS (ungarische Nr.3) (R late 1944 ?, destroyed February 1945)

33. Waffen-Grenadier-Division der SS 'Charlemagne' (französische Nr.1) (DS early 1945)

34. SS-Freiwilligen-Grenadier-Division 'Landstorm Nederland' (DS September 1944)

35. SS- und Polizei-Grenadier-Division (DS February 1945)

36. Waffen-Grenadier-Division der SS (DS early 1945 ?)

37. SS-Freiwilligen-Kavallerie-Division 'Lützow' (R February 1945)

38. SS-Grenadier-Division 'Nibelungen' (R March 1945)

This SS-Unterscharführer (equivalent to a senior corporal or junior sergeant) wears an Army-style M1936 tunic with a dark green 'badge-cloth' collar. The single silver pip on the left collar patch identifies his rank, and the collar Tresse his senior NCO status. The patch on his right collar is the rampant lion motif adopted in 1944 for the Ukrainian or 'Galician' 14.Waffen-Grenadier-Division der SS.

This SS-Unterscharführer wears the field-grey special uniform for self-propelled armoured assault artillery and tank-destroyer crews; NCO collar Tresse was not normally worn on this garment. Note the non-regulation use of two eagles on his M1943 field cap - the usual cloth badge above the death's-head on the front, and a metal badge on the left side.

⚡⚡ WAFFENFARBE

As in the Army and the Air Force, personnel of the various arms and branches of service within the Waffen-SS were visibly distinguished by the use of *Waffenfarbe* (branch colours) on the uniform. In the Waffen-SS these appeared as piping round the edges of the shoulder straps of non-commissioned ranks, and as underlay - in conjunction with a second black underlay - on officers' shoulder straps.

Initially all personnel of the original SS-Verfügungstruppe combat units, and the Totenkopf internal security regiments, wore white Waffenfarbe - the Army's traditional colour for infantry. (The division between the two organisations was maintained throughout the war. Some Totenkopf units were transferred to the combat arm in November 1939 and subsequently. The term Waffen-SS, embracing all combat units, was introduced in December 1939, but did not definitively replace the earlier SS-VT designation until April 1941.)

On 10 May 1940 the adoption of different branch-coloured pipings and underlays on shoulder straps was ordered, to be completed by 31 December 1940; however, some individuals retained white on the shoulder straps throughout the war. For the short currency of another clause of the same order, rescinded on 5 November 1940, branch-coloured pipings were also authorised for use on the crown seam and band edges of the peaked service cap, and on the side seams of the undress trousers. Again, many individuals seem to have retained these long after permission was officially withdrawn.

The following list shows the colours authorised for the main branches under the May 1940 orders, with changes and additions ordered at varying dates during the war years.

White *(weiss)* Infantry, Totenkopf, Grenadier & Panzer-Grenadier units
Light grey *(hellgrau)* 'Main offices' (higher command departments); and general officers
Dark grey *(dunkelgrau)* Personal staff of the Reichsführer-SS (Himmler)
Black *(schwarz)* Engineers; construction units (Pionier- & Bau-einheiten)

Lemon yellow *(zitronengelb)* Signals; propaganda troops (war correspondents)
Golden yellow *(goldgelb)* Cavalry; reconnaissance (Aufklärungs) units post-June 1942
Copper brown *(kupferbraun)* Reconnaissance (Aufklärungs) units, pre-June 1942
Light brown *(hellbraun)* Concentration camp (KL) service - not part of the Waffen-SS, but listed here for elimination, since uniform items with Totenkopf insignia may be confused with those associated with e.g. the Waffen-SS Division 'Totenkopf'.

Pink *(rosa)* Tank (Panzer); anti-tank (Panzer-Abwehr); and tank-destroyer (Panzerjäger) units
Light pink *(hellrosa)* Transport service/troops
Light salmon pink *(hell-lachrosa)* Military geologists

Orange *(orangerot)* Military police (Feldgendarmerie); special services (recruiting & replacement; ordnance, vehicle, signals etc specialists)
Bright red *(hochrot)* Artillery; Flak (anti-aircraft) units
Crimson *(karmesinrot)* Veterinary service
Bordeaux red *(Bordeauxrot)* Legal service; rocket units (Werfer-einheiten)

Red & grey twist cord *(rot-grau)* Specialists (Fachführer) post-June 1942

Light blue *(hellblau)* Transport and supply units; field post office personnel
Sky blue *(lichtblau)* Administration service
Dark 'cornflower' blue *(kornblumenblau)* Medical personnel

Light or 'meadow' green *(hellgrün, wiesengrün)* Mountain (Gebirgs) troops; rifle regts of the SS-Polizei-Division pre-1942
Dark green *(dunkelgrün)* Reserve officers; specialists (Fachführer) pre-June 1942
Toxic green *(giftgrün)* Security service (Sicherheitsdienst, SD)

WAFFEN-⚡⚡ RANKS

The British/American equivalent ranks given below are in many cases only approximate; the German armed forces had a larger number of separate grades, both of general officers and of NCOs and warrant officers.

General officers:

Reichsführer-SS	National Leader (Heinrich Himmler)
SS-Oberstgruppenführer	Colonel-General
SS-Obergruppenführer	General
SS-Gruppenführer	Lieutenant-General
SS-Brigadeführer	Major-General
SS-Oberführer	Brigadier-General

Field officers:

SS-Standartenführer	Colonel
SS-Obersturmbannführer	Lieutenant-Colonel
SS-Sturmbannführer	Major

Company officers:

SS-Hauptsturmführer	Captain
SS-Obersturmführer	1st Lieutenant
SS-Untersturmführer	2nd Lieutenant

Warrant officers & senior NCOs:

SS-Sturmscharführer	Warrant Officer
SS-Hauptscharführer	Sergeant-Major
SS-Oberscharführer	Staff Sergeant
SS-Scharführer	Sergeant
SS-Unterscharführer	Lance-Sergeant

Junior NCOs & troops:

SS-Rottenführer	Corporal
SS-Sturmann	Lance-Corporal
SS-Oberschütze, -Obergrenadier, etc.	Senior Private
SS-Schütze, -Grenadier, etc. (generically, **SS-Mann**)	Private

SS-Obersturmbannführer Hans Dorr wearing officer's service dress cap and tunic, displaying the Knight's Cross with Swords and Oakleaves. His officer status is shown by the silver cord edging to his collar patches; his rank is shown on his left hand patch by four pips and a double line of braid, all in silver. Dorr commanded the 'Germania' regiment of the 5.SS-Panzer-Division 'Wiking'.

SS-Standartenführer Otto Kumm won the Oakleaves to his Knight's Cross in April 1943 as commander of the 'Der Führer' regiment of the SS-Panzer-Grenadier-Division 'Das Reich'. From this rank - full colonel - upwards, rank insignia were worn on both collar patches. In 1944 Kumm commanded the 'Prinz Eugen' Division, and in 1945, briefly, the 'Leibstandarte SS Adolf Hitler'.

HEADGEAR
General officer's service cap

In 1937 an officer's peaked service cap (Schirmmütze) was introduced, following the design of the black cap worn with the black Allgemeine-SS service uniform. However, in line with the introduction of the field-grey service uniform this cap had a field-grey 'pavilion' (crown). The cap band was in black velvet for officer grades, and had a doubled silver bullion chin cord.

(Above) **Caps for general officers showed silver bullion piping at the crown seam and the top and bottom edges of the band, regardless of branch of service. This example is manufactured by the prestigious firm of 'Erel' (an acronym of the initials 'RL' for the owner, Robert Lubstein). It is constructed from a fine grade grey wool and exhibits the highest standards of workmanship. The standard SS pattern national eagle and death's-head badges are here made in stamped aluminium.**

(Right) **The lining is of a bronze-coloured artificial silk, with a celluloid sweatshield and a brown leather sweatband. The lining under the sweatshield is impressed with the maker's logo and 'Offizier Kleiderkasse', meaning that this item was officially sanctioned by the officers' clothing outlet (official supplier to Wehrmacht officers). The cap is also impressed on the sweatband 'Erel Stirnschütze', indicating that it is ventilated at the forehead area by perforating the sweatband with small ventilation holes and backing it with an orange-coloured sponge material.**

General officer's service cap

Generals, and indeed all other officers, were responsible for procuring their own uniforms and accoutrements; the financial burden was lessened by the provision of an allowance and coupons redeemable on items available from the Kleiderkasse (or clothing fund outlet). Many different qualities and materials will therefore be encountered between different examples of the same items.

(Above) **This general officer's peaked service cap is constructed using a fine grey ribbed tricot material, and displays features found on less expensive grade caps. The silver general officer's piping, the black velvet band, and the silver bullion chin cord with bullion slides and 13mm pebble-finish silver buttons, are all conventional. On this example the national eagle and swastika badge and the SS death's-head insignia are made from steel finished with a silver wash.**

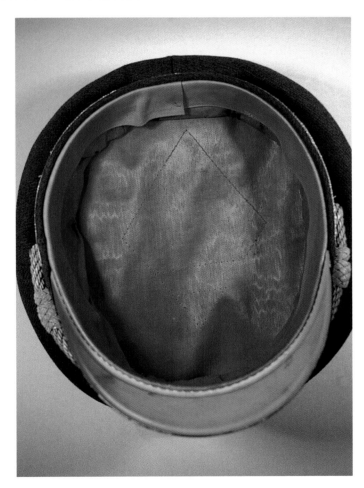

(Right) **The lining is made from a watered silk; it has a celluloid sweatshield in a diamond shape, with no manufacturer's logo. This shape of sweatshield is normally associated with less expensive caps (in contrast to the marked 'rounded top' shields). The sweatband is also of a thinner, less expensive leather.**

Officer's service cap

This example has a fine grey wool crown and black velvet band, and displays the usual features of a Waffen-SS officer's cap. The white woollen piping is in accordance with regulation practice before the order of 10 May 1940 and after that of 5 November 1940. The badges on this example are made of materials encountered in the immediate pre-war and wartime periods: stamped in mild steel and finished with a silver wash. Prior to this badges can be found in aluminium, nickel silver and plated brass.

(Right) The badges worn on all Waffen-SS peaked caps consisted of the national eagle and swastika (Hoheitsabzeichen), and the death's-head (Totenkopf) of the SS. The national eagle was of a different design from the Army and Navy pattern, as the entire SS was regarded as a paramilitary force and thus not entitled to use the armed forces pattern; the most obvious characteristic of the SS pattern is the 'pointed' shape of the wings, with the longest feather in the centre. This pattern had replaced the smaller 'political' pattern of eagle in about 1936. Once adopted by the Allgemeine-SS and subsequently worn by the Waffen-SS, it remained unchanged in design until the end of the war. The design of death's-head illustrated had replaced a version without the lower jaw in around 1934.

Officer's service cap

Another example of a Waffen-SS officer's cap with the white Waffenfarbe piping, this one made from a grey ribbed tricot. It is interesting that this cap has had the internal stiffening spring removed to give it a more 'floppy' shape. Though against regulations, this was often done in the field in order to make the cap look less like a parade item and to give it the allure of a veteran's battlefield headgear. Though most frequent among junior officers and senior NCOs, this affectation can be seen in photographs of ranks from general to private.

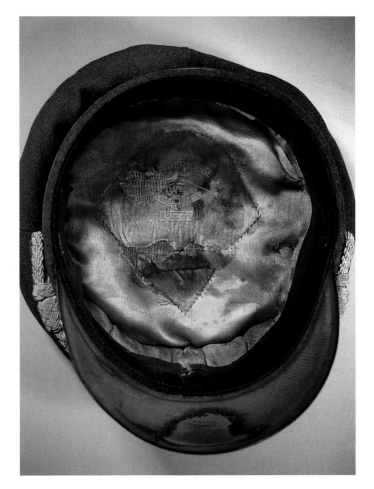

(Above) Another interesting feature is the use of the Army pattern national eagle rather than the SS pattern, which is occasionally seen in period photographs - due either to a simple lack of availability of the correct pattern, or to a wish to indicate an affiliation with the Army. Indeed, 'Sepp' Dietrich himself - commanding officer of the premier division 'Leibstandarte SS Adolf Hitler' - could often be seen wearing a peaked cap with a Heer (Army) pattern eagle badge. Occasionally Army pattern caps were also modified for use by the addition of a black velvet band and a death's-head badge.

(Right) The lining is constructed of a gold-coloured artificial silk which is heavily worn. The celluloid sweatshield is missing (these were often removed by the wearer for greater comfort), and impressed into this area is the logo of the manufacturer 'Erel'. Note the wear pattern in the centre underside of the peak, produced by the wearer's thumb grasping the same spot repeatedly when removing the cap.

KL officer's service cap

As mentioned above, Waffenfarbe cap piping in the wearers' branch colours other than white was permitted for a short period between 10 May and 5 November 1940, when a further order re-instated universal white; but despite this order, caps with coloured Waffenfarbe continued to be worn by many individuals until the end of the war. While this example - piped in the light brown Waffenfarbe of the concentration camp service - is not a Waffen-SS item, it is included here for comparison, and because it is identical to the officers' caps of the combat branches in style and construction.

(*Above*) A classic example of its type from the 'Erel' company, this cap has a field-grey crown in a fine ribbed twill and a black velvet band. The peak is made from the usual Vulkanfiber. The officer's chin cords are made from bullion wire and secured at each side with a 13mm stipple-finished button. This cap has mid-war quality badges in steel with a silver plating finish.

(*Right*) The lining is of a light green artificial silk material (often encountered from this manufacturer), and has a celluloid sweatshield. The sweatband is in brown leather, with a small white bow at the rear seam. The underside of the sweatshield and the sweatband are impressed with the maker's name.

Officer's adapted service cap

Due to the problems of obtaining some items during the war, and with the rapid promotion of non-commissioned soldiers to officer ranks, enlisted grade peaked service caps are often seen modified for use by officers. (To clarify the terms used for peaked or 'visored' service caps: Schirmmütze is a generic physical description, 'peaked cap', while Dienstmütze is a military term, 'service cap' referring to the orders of dress with which it was worn.)

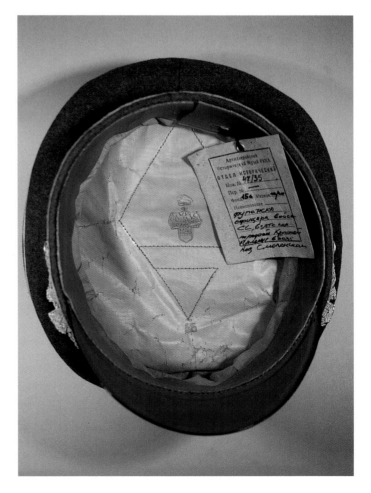

(Above) This example is essentially an enlisted/ NCO grade private purchase service cap (see pages 19-21) which has been adapted for use by an officer. By the addition of a silver bullion chin cord and side buttons, and by ignoring the black band being in wool rather than velvet, it was possible to keep an item in wear longer, saving materials and expense. It has a crown of field-grey wool (the finer texture and very green-grey colour suggesting an early example), and the black wool band. White wool piping may indicate an infantry unit, or simply the universal use of white by other branches, as explained above.

(Right) The lining is a textbook example of the enlisted mens' quality, made from orange oil-cloth material with a thin artificial leather sweat-band. That it is probably a private purchase item is indicated by a fine maker's imprint on the celluloid sweatshield.

The attached label from a Red Army museum in the USSR states that this is 'a cap of an SS officer, taken in the battle for Smolensk'.

Panzer officer's service cap

(*Above*) This cap shows the rose-pink piping of the Panzertruppe or armoured branch; the same colour Waffenfarbe was worn by anti-tank and self-propelled tank-destroyer units. Comparison of examples shows that the normal shade of the piping varied over time, from a deep rose pink in the early years to a softer pink from the middle war years on. It has the usual field-grey crown in a high quality wool material, the black velvet band and the doubled bullion chin cords. The insignia are of the early war silver plated steel variety, with the finish showing wear on the highlights from heavy use.

(*Right*) The lining is made from a bronze-coloured artificial silk and displays the maker's logo on the celluloid sweatshield. The soft brown leather sweatband has a velvet buffer strip between it and the body of the cap, a technique favoured by several manufacturers including Peter Küpper ('Peküro').

Officer's 'old model' field cap

This Offizierfeldmütze älterer Art, introduced in the Army in 1934 and officially superceded by the boat-shaped field cap in 1938 (on which occasion this 'old style' cap was so named for the first time), had no official equivalent in the Waffen-SS. Prior to an order of December 1939 that Waffen-SS officers should acquire a new field-grey field cap of Air Force pattern, individual officers seem to have privately purchased 'old style' field caps based on the Army model. This had a smaller crown than the service cap, and a soft leather peak; it was worn without chin cords or stiffener, and in the Army with flat machine-woven insignia - in the Waffen-SS such badges were not at first available, though they appeared later. Known to modern collectors as 'crusher' caps, these were extremely popular for their convenience, comfort, and rugged 'front line' appearance. In the pre-war SS-VT their use was probably inspired by the issue in 1938 of a similar but not identical field cap for NCOs (see page 18). The later promotion of numerous NCOs to officer rank may have contributed to the nonregulation retention of such caps by many officers.

(Above & below) **This example has a *feldgrau* wool crown of a quality indicative of wartime standards. The black band is of wool, as is the 'meadow-green' *(wiesengrün)* piping. The badges are early war production in stamped aluminium, polished to a shiny finish. Some wartime examples alternatively have BeVo woven badges. It has a brown liner, a brown sweatband, and does not have a sweatshield.**

NCO's M1938 field cap

This M1938 peaked field cap for NCOs (Feldmütze fur Unterführer) is manufactured in the original style, with a peak covered in the same cloth as the crown. The presence of copper-brown wool Waffenfarbe piping dates it to some time between May 1940, when piping in colours other than white was first permitted, and mid-1942, when the branch colour for reconnaissance troops was changed to golden yellow.

The fabric used in construction is a strong grey ribbed twill, with the usual black wool band. This example was probably privately ordered, as the orange oilcloth liner has a sweatshield – most 'crusher' caps will be found without one. The BeVo-woven eagle and death's-head are executed in white cotton and hand-sewn to the cap; many early examples show this method rather than machine sewing. As in the officer's version, the crown and peak lack stiffening.

Enlisted man's/NCO's service cap

The peaked Dienstmütze for enlisted ranks first appeared in 1939, and was initially for the use of senior NCOs in and near the barracks. Soon afterwards it became available to all enlisted ranks who wished to purchase it as a walking-out headgear. At least after the outbreak of the war, and probably earlier, it did not appear in the official lists of obligatory issue items.

(Above) This early cap is a conventional example, which is piped in white wool; note the appearance of the piping after losing its pile through long wear. The crown is made of material with a 'blueish' field-grey shade typical of early manufacture, and the band is black wool. The appearance of the crown is of the familiar wartime 'Sattelform' ('saddle shape'), as opposed to the pre-war 'Tellerform' ('plate shape'), which was distinctly flat and lacked the high, sweeping front. The chin strap is the early SS–VT pattern with a central link; the badges are in early quality silvered metal.

(Right) The lining is made from the orange oilcloth which was standard for enlisted ranks, with a silver imprint for the maker, Kurt Triebel of Kassel. Note that the celluloid sweatshield is missing. The rectangular stamp is a post-capture Russian archive marking, and the sweatband is possibly a replacement fitted by the Russian museum system.

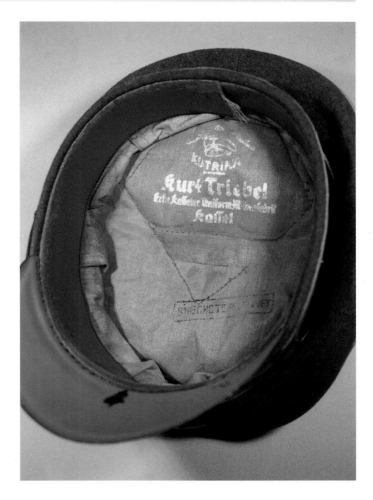

Cavalry NCO's service cap

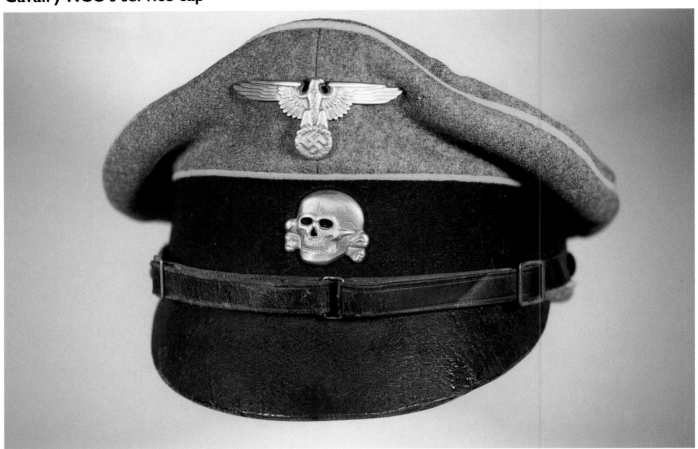

In the Waffen-SS, unlike the Army, senior NCOs were allowed to wear the peaked service cap while on duty at the front. This headgear thus became a sort of status symbol of senior rank, and photographic evidence shows NCOs wearing it very widely under most circumstances. Like their officers, individual NCOs often 'customised' the shape of the crown by removing the stiffener and pulling the sides down and the front up and back, which was felt to give it a more 'front line veteran' look.

(Above) This piece is a good example of this practice, and its battered allure is increased by its construction with the thick, soft leather peak normally associated with the officer's 'old style field cap'. It has a wartime *feldgrau* wool crown and a black wool band. The Waffenfarbe piping is in golden-yellow wool for the cavalry branch. The chin strap is the SS-VT style with a central link. The badges are of stamped aluminium.

(Right) The lining is made from grey twill, with no sweatshield but a tan brown sweatband. Under the peak a small stamp showing a Totenkopf above a pair of SS runes has been punched; its purpose or significance is unknown.

Panzer enlisted man's/NCO's service cap

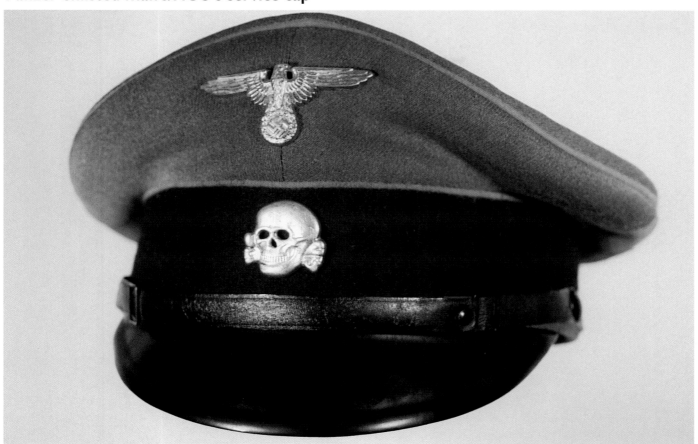

As previously noted, after the order of May 1940 allowed different Waffenfarbe cap piping colours, their use remained conventional practice despite being contrary to standing orders after November 1940. The colours identified the soldier at a glance as a member of a particular branch, and promoted a certain ésprit de corps. The display of non-regulation piping was more likely to be tolerated on an optional purchase item such as the service cap.

(Above) **This Panzer-truppe enlisted man's or NCO's peaked service cap is manufactured from a fine grade tricot, and the whole piece displays workmanship indicative of private purchase quality. The rose-pink wool piping identifies the armoured branch, and the cap band is made of a fine quality black wool. The badges are in a fine stamped nickel silver; the black patent leather chin strap is of the standard Wehrmacht pattern.**

(Right) **The lining is in keeping with that of a non-commissioned grade cap, as required by regulations. (Indeed, caps were often inspected at unit level and then stamped 'Geprüft' or 'checked' under the sweatband, signifying that they conformed to regulations.) This example has the standard orange oilcloth lining, but with a finer grade sweatband and a sweatshield bearing the imprint of the maker, Carl Halfar of Berlin.**

Officer's 'new model' field cap

The new model field cap for officers (Feldmütze fur Führer neuer Art) was introduced by an order of December 1939, to provide officers with a soft cap for field wear under conditions where the steel helmet was not required and the service cap was inconvenient the field cap could be stowed away easily if the helmet had to be put on. It was of the same pattern as the Luftwaffe's Fliegermütze: a 'boat-shaped' sidecap with a turned-up outer flap or curtain cut with a straight edge (in contrast to the Army officer's M1938 field cap, which had a 'scooped' cut-out at the front of the flap).

The cap illustrated was the personal property of SS-Sturmbannführer Alfred Arnold. After joining the SS in 1934 he served in the SS-VT, the Regiment 'Thule' of the 'Totenkopf' Division, the 'Nord' Division, with SS-Aufklärungs-Abteilung 1, and as one of the commanders of Panzer Brigade 'Gross'. He was killed in combat on 9 October 1944 in Latvia, after which he was posthumously awarded the German Cross in Gold. The authors are pleased to present his uniform and some other effects in this book for the first time in public.

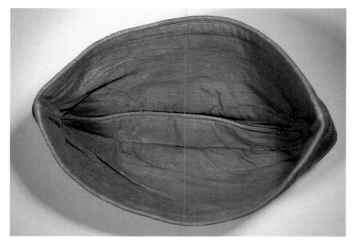

(*Above*) **Alfred Arnold's cap is made from a smooth grey tricot material and has a line of white piping around the turn-up. Some officers had silver piping fitted, but white Waffenfarbe was officially supposed to be worn regardless of the branch; as on the service cap, the regulation was widely ignored. The BeVo machine-woven badges in grey and off-white cotton** are hand-sewn to the cap; it is interesting that they are not of the regulation silver bullion pattern for officers.

(*Upper right*) **The snapshot shows Arnold wearing this actual cap during the campaign in France, while serving with the 'Totenkopf' Division in the rank of SS-Hauptsturmführer.**

Enlisted man's/NCO's 'new model' field cap

(Left) The example shown here is a high quality cap, and is probably a private purchase piece. This is reflected in the standard of materials alone - the cut and construction are exactly as per regulation issue. The body is made here from a fine grey melton wool; issue examples are made from the same coarser *feldgrau* wool as tunics and trousers. The BeVo-woven badges on this cap are standard issue and have been machine-sewn to the front of the crown and turn-up during construction; hand-sewn insignia are not uncommon, however.

The Feldmütze neuer Art für Mannschaften was introduced for wear by an order of 1 November 1940. It replaced all previous SS-VT style caps; and was issued to all troops until replaced in autumn 1943 by the Einheitsfeldmütze Modell 1943 peaked field cap. Like the officer's version the enlisted ranks' M1940 '*Schiffchen*' ('little boat') was a sidecap with a straight-edged turn-up flap, following the equivalent Luftwaffe design. (The turn-up flap was theoretically intended to be folded down for extra protection in bad weather, but photographs only very rarely show it worn in this fashion.) Panzer troops were issued the same cap in black wool.

Initially, as a carry-over from the pre-war SS-VT sidecap, the Waffen-SS followed Army practice in adding a soutache (inverted 'V') of Waffenfarbe-coloured Russia braid enclosing the death's-head badge. This is seen in photographs, but not very often, and the practice was ordered discontinued in September 1942. The death's-head being larger than the Army's national cockade, fitting the braid neatly around it was more difficult.

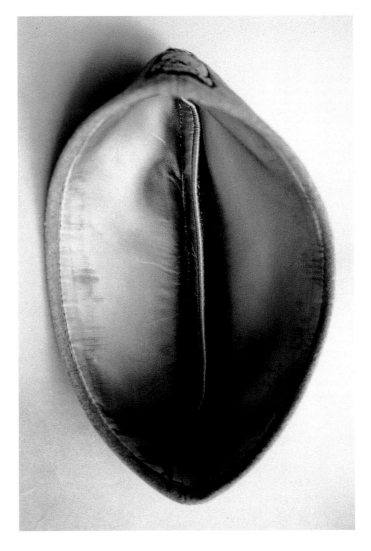

(Opposite) The lining of Arnold's cap is made from a grey cotton drill material and there are no visible markings. This cap is a very large size 60.

(Right) This private purchase cap has a silver-grey artificial silk lining; issue examples will be found with linings of grey-brown cotton or cotton drill. Some issue caps carry size and/or manufacturers' markings, but often display neither.

Officer's mountain cap

The mountain troops of the Waffen-SS were issued with the Army-style Bergmütze from October 1940. At the time this very practical form of headdress was unique to mountain units; its origins lay in the M1907/08 field service cap worn by Austrian troops during the First World War. It provided protection from the elements and shaded the eyes, was comfortable, and could be stowed away easily. The Bergmütze proved so popular and successful that it was used as the basis for the universal field cap introduced for the Army, Luftwaffe and Waffen-SS in 1943.

(Above) **This officer's example is made from fine quality wool of the early 'blue-grey' shade of field-grey. The turn-up flap around the body can be lowered to protect the neck and face, and this is secured with two standard stipple-finish buttons (though the buttons on this example are slightly larger than normal). Buttons may be found in metal, horn, or a cast resin material. The crown of the cap is piped in silver bullion cord; this was ordered as an officers' distinction on the Army mountain cap on** 3 October 1942, and the Waffen-SS seems to have quickly followed suit. The officer's quality silver wire BeVo death's-head badge is worn on the front of the crown.

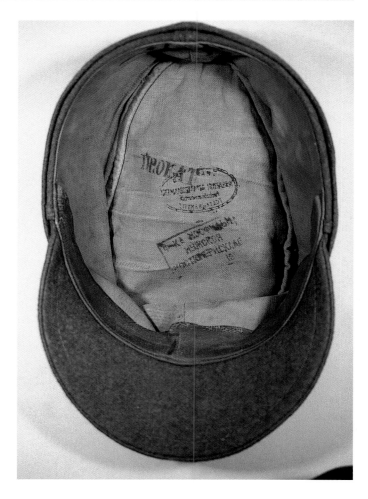

(Right) The lining is made from a hard-wearing cotton drill; today it exhibits a maker's stamp in black, and Russian museum stamps in purple. There is a leather sweatband covering the forehead area of the lining - an indication of an officer's quality cap.

[Left] A particularly nice example of the officer's quality bullion Edelweiss badge of the Waffen-SS mountain troops is sewn to the left side above the ear (the Army equivalent was produced only in metal).

[Right] The officer's Bergmütze worn with an officer's tunic of the 7th SS Volunteer Mountain Division 'Prinz Eugen' - see also pages 50-51.

Officer's M1943 field cap

During 1943 the Wehrmacht made the practical decision to attempt a standardisation of clothing across the board. One of the most popular items introduced was the Model 1943 universal field cap (Einheitsfeldmütze), which was ordered into production to replace the sidecaps of the Army, Waffen-SS and Luftwaffe as field headgear. The sidecap was felt to provide inadequate protection, and the popular mountain cap was adopted as the model for the new headgear. In the case of the Waffen-SS the order was dated 1 October 1943. The new peaked field cap, with silver piping around the crown seam as a distinction, was soon widely adopted by officers.

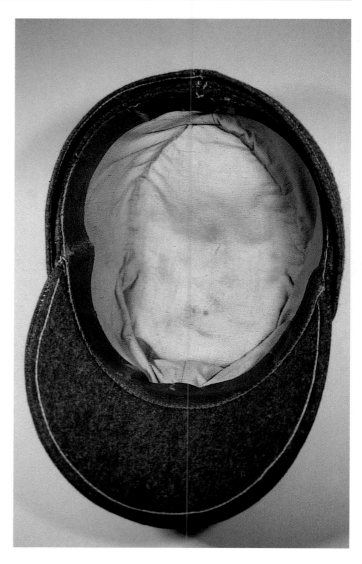

(*Above*) The officer's cap illustrated is an example of the last pattern of M1943 Einheitsfeldmütze introduced during the war. It is constructed of a rough *feldgrau* wool with a high synthetic content. The peak of all M1943 caps is noticeably longer, and the crown noticeably lower, than those of the Bergmütze. The crown of the cap is piped in silver-coloured cord, this being the only external mark of officer status.

Early M1943 caps had separate BeVo badges: the death's-head sewn to the front of the crown, and the eagle - for lack of space above it - on the left side of the turn-up flap. The pattern of combined insignia illustrated here was the very last introduced. It was produced in both BeVo machine-weave and this rather cruder machine-embroidered pattern, but not to officer's quality in silver wire. This single-piece pattern was worn by all ranks, although individual officers replaced it in various ways. Note also that some late pattern caps have a single flap button rather than two.

(*Right*) The lining is made here from a light grey cotton, and a sweatband made from thin *ersatz* leather is fitted - a feature generally found only in officers' caps.

Enlisted man's/NCO's M1943 field cap

This cap is a good example of the sort of variations in insignia that could be encountered, especially within foreign volunteer units. Caps were often issued to such units from secondhand depot stocks, and consequently a wide variety of insignia might be encountered. Soldiers also sought to personalise their uniforms, often obtaining items from outside sources and replacing various pieces of insignia. For instance, many photographs show Waffen-SS soldiers wearing the metal death's-head badge from the peaked service cap on the field cap - an entirely unofficial practice.

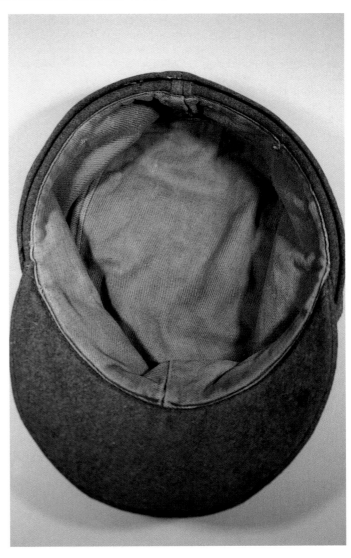

(Above) This cap is a very ordinary example of the standard M1943 Einheitsfeldmütze made in wool of an early-looking grey-green shade. The front flap is secured by two pressed paper buttons - these are most likely replacements for lost buttons. The interesting feature is the anachronistic death's-head badge of woven wool, which has clearly been cut from a 'Totenkopf' Division right hand collar patch; note that it incorrectly faces to the right as viewed. This adaptation - though normally using the correct, left-facing death's-head - has been observed on peaked caps, sidecaps and the M1943 cap. The cap illustrated does not exhibit the second, national eagle badge.

(Right) The lining is in a heavy grey drill material, and shows no visible markings.

Panzer enlisted man's/NCO's M1943 field cap

Field caps issued to tank crews for wear with their black vehicle uniform followed those produced for other branches in field-grey, but were made from black wool. The October 1943 order for the production of the Waffen-SS Einheitsfeldmütze specified both field grey and black versions. This cap was standard after 1943, and became almost universal as heavy casualties were replaced by men who received it as their original issue. It was not as popular among Panzer personnel, however, since the peak interfered with the use of optical equipment. It could always be turned backwards, of course; but those crews who already had them tried to hold onto their black sidecaps for as long as possible.

(Above) This example is made from a heavy, high quality black wool. The shoulder strap tabs under the turn-up flap are made from the same material. The flap is secured with a pair of 12mm stipple-finish buttons. Many late war caps used black bakelite buttons instead, and there was a version with a single button. The one-piece insignia is the BeVo machine-woven variant of the last pattern issued during the war; as with the field grey cap, there is also a wool-embroidered version. Again, officers' caps as manufactured were distinguished only by silver piping around the crown seam, although individuals sometimes replaced the insignia with separate officer-quality badges of earlier pattern.

(Right) The lining is cut from a heavy grey denim twill and carries some faint stamped markings, but these have been obscured by a later Russian museum acquisition number.

Another feature encountered in some SS Panzer caps is an exposed underside to the peak. This so-called 'Dachau'-style cap (from the fact that American soldiers took many as souvenirs from a clothing depot located close to the notorious camp) shows the cardboard stiffener on the underside, rather than the complete wool covering seen on this example; such caps are the exception rather than the rule, however.

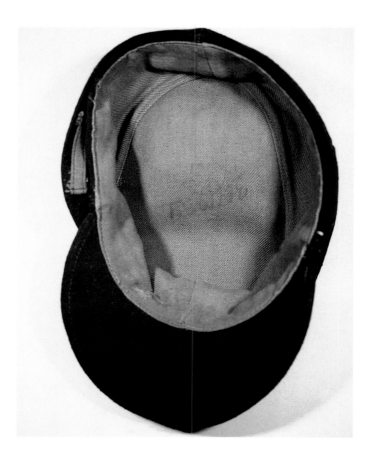

M1918 double-decal helmet

In the pre-war period the organisations which would later be brought together as the Waffen-SS used both M1916 and M1918 pattern steel helmets; indeed, these First World War models were still seen in service even after the M1935 became available. (In this context 'M1918' refers not to the pattern with cut-outs over the ears, but to the type illustrated here, which differed from the M1916 only in details of the rivets and chin strap.) They were used during the Polish and French campaigns of 1939 and 1940; and later were often issued to foreign volunteer units if there was a shortage of the M1935. Due to shortfalls in supply the Reichszeugmeisterei (RZM) also had their own copy of this helmet made, but with solid metal rivets instead of split brad pins. Stamped on either side of the inner flange with the SS runes and an RZM logo, such helmets are extremely rare. This pattern of helmet was regarded as less than ballistically protective, and reserved for parade duties only.

(Above) **This example of the 1918 modification to the M1916 pattern has been finished in field-grey paint and has had a set of first pattern (September 1935) SS runic and national/party decals applied.**

(Right) **The first pattern runes decal applied to the right side of the helmet is recognisable by its thin black border. More noticeably, each rune is distinctly formed by two separate strokes, 'overlapping' for only about half their width, the central points being very sharply cut at acute angles. These decals are extremely thin, and when viewed with the light across them they appear to be simply part of the paint surface rather than having been applied on top.**

Camouflaged M1942 single-decal helmet

Issue of the new M1935 helmet progressed gradually after its introduction into service with the 'Leibstandarte' in 1936. Eventually all Waffen-SS troops would be issued with the new helmet and the older patterns were withdrawn to depot for stockpiling or re-issue. From this time on the Waffen-SS would be issued with the same helmet as the Army, progressing through the M1935 and M1940 to the final M1942 pattern. The M1942 was basically the same as the previous two models apart from the finishing of the edge of the bowl; for economy reasons this was left 'raw' and flared outwards, rather than being crimped over as with the M1935 and M1940 patterns.

In the field the realities of combat required the dulling of the helmet's previously shiny surface; for the same reason, in March 1940 the national/party decal previously applied to the left side was ordered removed. In France that spring many troops could be observed with their helmets daubed with mud; and on the Eastern Front especially, soldiers took it upon themselves to camouflage their helmets with anything available, from vehicle paint to whitewash in winter.

(Above) **This M1942 has been painted - with impressive care - in at least three different colours, in a style intended to mimic the 1944-issue 'Dot' pattern camouflage clothing. Note that the second pattern runic decal has been neatly painted around; and yet that the helmet was painted while covered with chickenwire netting, the pattern of which shows in the paint. This wire was used over helmets when a fabric cam-** **ouflage cover was unavailable, to allow the fixing of local foliage. These browns, greens and ochres were the colours issued to camouflage vehicles from mid-1943 onwards.**

(Right) **This particular helmet, which was recovered in Latvia, has the owner's initials painted on the underside of the rear flange. Note that the chin strap was missing and the one shown, while original, is a replacement.**

M1942 single-decal helmet

(Above) **Although the national/party decal was ordered out of use before the May 1940 Blitzkreig campaign in the West, photographs suggest that many individuals ignored this ruling until the supply of decals was exhausted. However, this M1942 helmet finished with the typical grey wartime paint has only a single runic decal of the second pattern.**

(Upper right) **This helmet is also marked under the back flange with the owner's name in white paint. This was a common practice, and various levels of skill will be found, from 'signwriter' quality lettering to the downright crude. This helmet was apparently worn by SS-Scharführer P.Krüger of the 43rd SS Grenadier Regiment. The full unit title was Waffen-Grenadier- Regiment der SS 43 'Hinrich Schuldt', part of the Latvian 19.Waffen-Grenadier-Division der SS (lettische Nr.2), which fought on the Baltic sector of the Russian Front in 1944-45.**

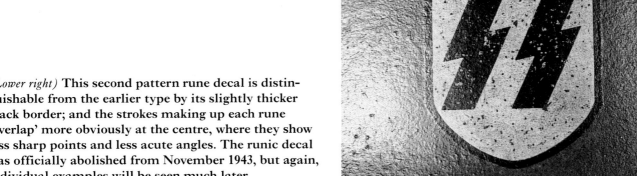

(Lower right) **This second pattern rune decal is distinguishable from the earlier type by its slightly thicker black border; and the strokes making up each rune 'overlap' more obviously at the centre, where they show less sharp points and less acute angles. The runic decal was officially abolished from November 1943, but again, individual examples will be seen much later.**

'Plane tree' camouflage helmet cover

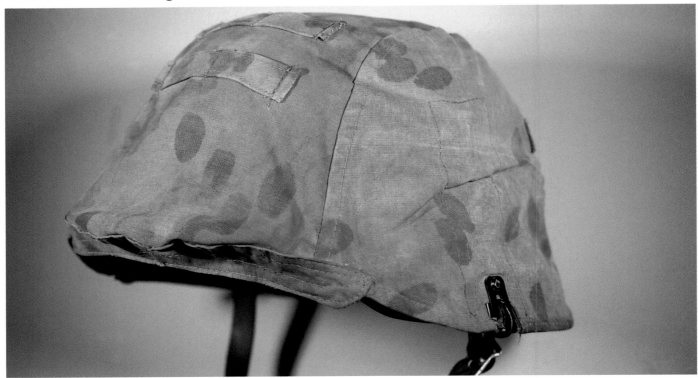

The Waffen-SS were the first military organisation to introduce camouflage-printed combat clothing as general issue. One of the first items, tested in late 1937 and awarded a patent in June 1938, was the camouflage helmet cover (Tarnhelmüberzug). In the trenches of the First World War the French Army had briefly issued a plain drab cloth helmet cover during the first months of 1916, but this was discontinued. The M1937 Waffen-SS item was designed with much greater inegenuity. The cover was made from three panels of a tough cotton duck material so as to hug the contours of the helmet. It was held on by an 'envelope' of material that slipped over the peak, and by three small sprung 'rocker' clips, one on either side and one at the rear. These clips where hinged so that the reversible cover could be attached with either side exposed. The fabric was printed on both sides in contrasting 'seasonal' colour schemes for spring/summer and autumn/winter.

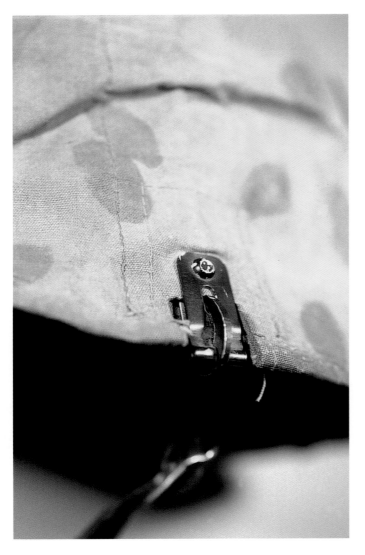

(*Above & left*) **The cover illustrated, here with the predominantly green 'spring/summer' side exposed, is a typical mid- to late-war example. Interestingly, it is made from pieces of cloth showing two different formats of the 'Plane tree' camouflage pattern (so-called from its resemblance to plane tree bark). Several minor variations are known, and as the covers were made from off-cuts of material left over after the construction of** smocks and other large items, the use of more than one pattern in a single cover is often encountered. Note also the detail of the blackened aluminium 'rocker' clip.

(*Opposite*) **The cover reversed to show the 'autumn/winter' side. The green side was always dominant; where any hems are folded over it is always a strip of the green side which is seen edging the brown, never vice-versa.**

'Plane tree' camouflage helmet cover

'Plane tree' camouflage helmet cover

'Plane tree' camouflage helmet cover

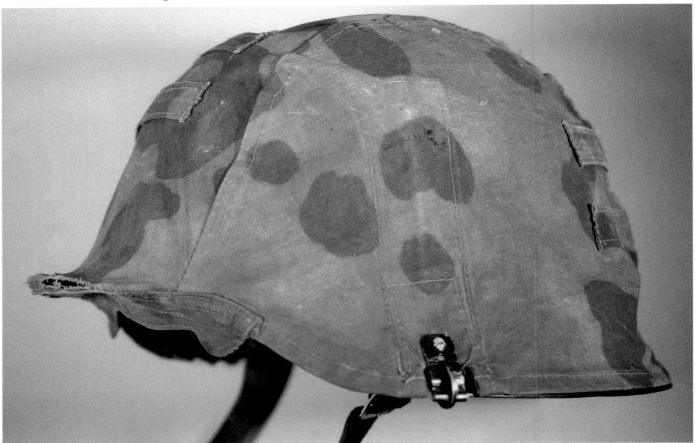

Helmet covers produced from the time of introduction in 1938 until 1941 were smooth on the surface and devoid of attachments. Recognising the value of local foliage for further concealment, however, the Waffen-SS then introduced the so-called second pattern cover, with several strips of the same cloth sewn in loops around the outside to allow temporary attachment of local grass and leaves. Six strips in three pairs were sewn high up at equal intervals around the cover, at the front and well back on each side.

This example is also in a 'Plane tree' pattern, with a rather faded spring/summer side (above) and an even less distinct pattern on the autumn/winter side (opposite). Note the way in which the front lip or envelope of the cover (right) is reinforced with several rows of lateral stitching.

(*Opposite above*) Observe also the vertical doubling strip of fabric which covers the tension spring for the retainer clips; these springs kept the cover snugged tightly down all over the helmet. Such care and expense in the production of an item as essentially simple as a helmet cover set the Waffen-SS apart from the German Army, whose covers were simple drawstring-fastened 'bags'.

(*Opposite below*) The foliage loops are attached very simply; these were simply scraps of material rolled into a doubled strip and sewn in place at each end and roughly in the centre, leaving the ends raw and unfinished.

'Plane tree' camouflage helmet cover

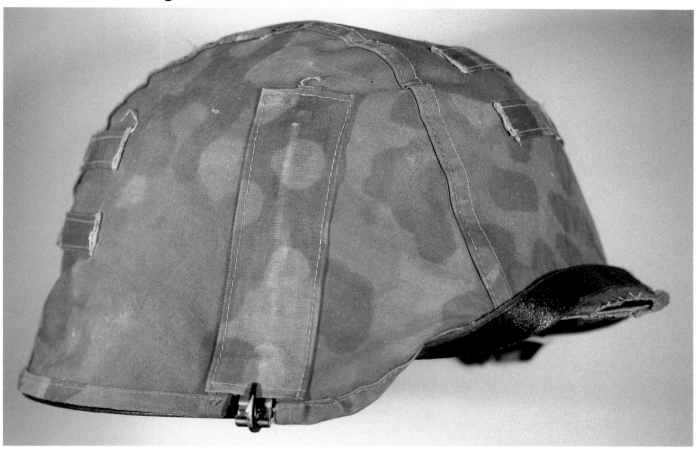

'Plane tree' camouflage helmet cover

'Plane tree' camouflage helmet cover

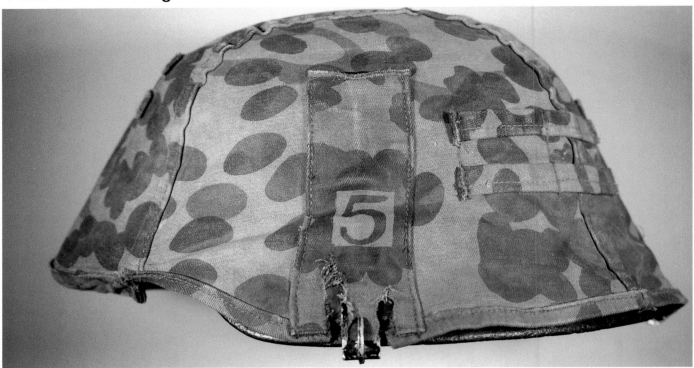

The main patterns of printed camouflage schemes are known to collectors (and in at least some cases, were probably known to their manufacturers as well) as 'Plane tree', 'Palm', 'Oakleaf', 'Blurred Edge' and 'Dot'. Considerable photographic research has been devoted to identifying the periods during which these were manufactured and the range of items for which each was used. (Note that the 'Dot 44' pattern was not employed for helmet covers, Zeltbahns or field caps). Within each of these patterns, especially 'Plane tree' and 'Oakleaf', many slight variations are encountered, due to manufacture by different companies and the use of differing dye batches.

The panels of 'Plane tree' camouflage are often found to incorporate a printed numeral as part of each design, from '1' to '6'. These have been the subject of much debate. Some researchers believe that they enabled the panels to be joined in a continuous, flowing pattern during manufacture; others, that they are associated with the manufacture of the Waffen-SS camouflage tent section, and were intended as a guide to the buttoning together of matching tent sections in the field; still others, that they were the identifying/register marks of the successive printing screens applied to the fabric during the printing process.

(Above) **Whatever the explanation, this 'Plane tree' second pattern cover shows the number '5' prominently at the side; it is illustrated on this page on the autumn/winter side - which is printed in a much more distinct scheme than that on page 35.**

(Right & opposite) **Again, note the 'rocker' clip for attachment and its tensioning spring above. This aluminium clip has the usual black-painted finish, although late manufacture examples often have unpainted steel clips.**

(Opposite above) **The excellently defined pattern on the spring/summer side of this 'Plane tree' cover.**

(Opposite below) **The predominantly brown side of the cover worn in conjunction with a smock showing the autumn/winter side of one of the 'Oakleaf' patterns (see also pages 86-87). The use together of different patterns of helmet cover and smock was commonplace.**

'Plane tree' camouflage helmet cover

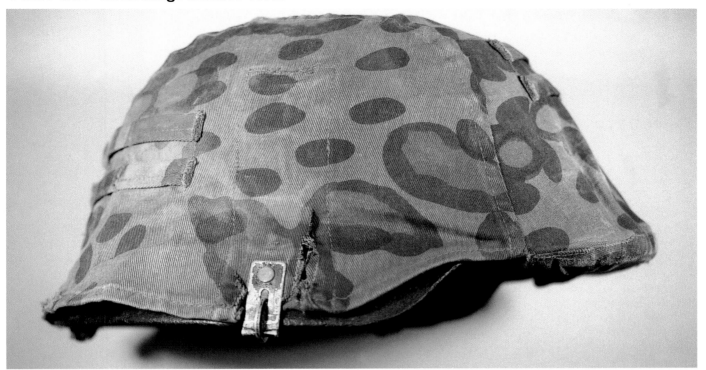

SERVICE UNIFORMS

General's service tunic

This tunic was the personal property of SS-Gruppenführer Lothar Debes. A First World War veteran, Debes joined the SS in 1937, at a time when many Army officers were transferring to a service in which a shortage of professional soldiers promised swift promotion. He commanded the SS-Junkerschule Braunschweig until 1942, then the 9.SS-Infanterie-Brigade, later becoming commandant of the

Waffen-SS officers' academy, the SS-Junkerschule at Bad Tölz. In 1943 he commanded the 'Frundsberg' Division (at that time titled 'Karl der Grosse') during its formation. From January to May 1944 he commanded the 6th SS Mountain Division 'Nord' on the Finnish front. Debes served in senior administrative positions from mid-1944 until the end of the war; he died in July 1960.

The tunic is cut in the pre-war style, with pleated patch breast pockets and slanted lower pockets, and made from a very fine field-green wool material. The front edge and turn-back cuffs are piped in dove grey, the Waffenfarbe of Waffen-SS general officers. The collar, of dark green 'badge cloth', is secured with three sets of hooks-&-eyes. Note also the many sets of worked thread loops on the left breast for the attachment of pin-back awards.

(Left) This photograph shows SS-Gruppenführer Debes (second from right) in spring 1944 when he was commanding general of 6.SS-Gebirgs-Division 'Nord' on the Finnish sector of the Russian Front. The officer at first right is Alfred Arnold, Gen Debes' adjutant during this period. Arnold's uniform is presented on pages 42–45.

The lining is made from steel-grey rayon, having a slash pocket inside the left breast. There are two labels to the firm of Traugott Rahne of Hannover: one BeVo-woven label on the outside (see below), and another fabric label on the inside of the left breast pocket (see right). This second label is dated 10 September 1942 and names the owner as 'Brigadeführer L.Debes', his rank at that time. There is a strap under the left armpit for suspension of a dress dagger or sword, and a slot inside the outer pocket for this to pass through. The sleeves are lined in a striped material, commonly found in lined tunics.

(Top) **Rank insignia consist of a pair of post-1941 SS-Gruppenführer collar patches in silver bullion weave on black velvet with silver cord edging. Before 1942 this rank, equivalent to lieutenant-general, was identified by the triple oakleaves without the additional 'pip'. Note the particularly tall collar of this tunic.**

(Above) **The SS-style national eagle-and-swastika badge on the left sleeve is hand-embroidered in silver bullion wire over a** cardboard template. It was also available in a flat silver machine-woven (BeVo) pattern. This quality was not peculiar to generals but was available to all officer ranks.

(Right) The shoulder straps of this rank did not change post-1941. For all grades of Waffen-SS general officers they consisted of one silver intertwined between two gold cords on a dove-grey underlay. Exact rank was indicated by one, two and three 26mm silver 'pips'.

Panzer officer's service uniform

This uniform was the property of SS-Sturmbannführer Alfred Arnold. Arnold was a senior officer in the temporary tactical formation designated Panzer Brigade Gross when he was killed in action in Latvia on 9 October 1944; his earlier career is outlined on page 22, and his decorations are illustrated on page 125. While it appears from photographic evidence that he owned several combat uniforms, this tunic, which is in the old-style cut, is assumed to have been kept for walking-out or dress wear. Use of the pre-war pattern uniform was regarded as a sign of 'veteran' status.

The tunic is finely tailored in the pre-war fashion, having box-pleated patch breast pockets and slanted lower slash pockets covered by flaps. This pattern was introduced into the Waffen-SS in 1937, replacing the old earth-grey field uniform. It also mimics exactly the cut of the old-style Army officer's service tunic. It has deep turn-back cuffs on the sleeves, and the collar is in dark green badge cloth cut in the elongated, acute points which were thought fashionable. Several worked thread loops are provided for the attachment of awards. Photographs indicate that Arnold wore only a ribbon bar and Iron Cross 1st Class and alternated between wearing his Infantry Assault Badge or the silver grade Wound Badge.

The lining (see page 44) is in steel-grey rayon with a pocket inside the left breast. The front is fitted with an internal waistbelt to promote a more flattering fit. The usual dagger hanger is fitted under the left armpit, with an opening through which it may be passed to emerge under the outer pocket flap. The sleeves are lined with the usual striped material.

(Left) Alfred Arnold is seen here in 1944 recuperating in hospital from wounds received in battle; he would be killed shortly afterwards. He wears here the actual tunic illustrated in colour on these pages; compare the enlisted grade sleeve eagle, the depth of the pocket flaps and their alignment with the buttons, and the pressing wear to the top of the turn-back cuff.

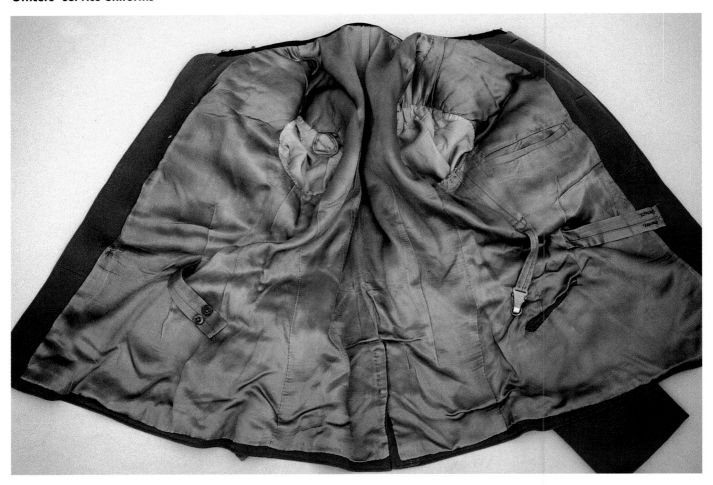

(*Centre*) Inside the interior tunic pocket is an impregnated cloth tailor's label from Max Maetzulat of Friedrichstrasse, Berlin; it is named to 'SS-Hauptsturmführer Arnold A' and dated November 1942.

(*Left*) Field-grey breeches which belonged to Arnold, as worn by Waffen-SS and Army officers; note the three-button calf closure, for a snug fit. They have a buttoning slash pocket at each hip, one on the right rear, and an open fob pocket at right front. Both braces (suspender) buttons and belt loops are provided.

(*Above*) The label inside the breeches, from N.Keidenreich & Söhne of München (Munich), gives the owner as 'Hptstf.Arnold' and the date as May 1943.

(Top) The collar patches show the standard officers' configuration: on the wearer's right are a pair of finely hand-embroidered silver bullion SS-runes *(Sigrunen, Doppelrunen)*, and on the left the four 'pips' indicating the rank of SS-Sturmbannführer.

(Above) Interestingly, Arnold did not wear the usual officer grade sleeve eagle in silver bullion, but rather a machine-embroidered enlisted ranks' pattern. This is unusual on a tailored tunic, but period photographs (e.g. see page 43) confirm its use. This was probably due simply to a temporary shortage of officers' type eagles.

(Right) The shoulder straps are sewn into the shoulder seams. Officers' rank straps followed the Army system, with interwoven silver cords for field ranks, on a Waffenfarbe underlay - here, unusually, the pink of Panzer troops is displayed in rayon rather than wool - but with a second base underlay in black for all branches.

Officer's adapted service tunic, 'Nord' Division

Officers were permitted to draw an enlisted ranks' service tunic from unit stores once a year free of charge, and to have them upgraded for field use in order to save wear on their more expensive tailored tunics. This is a perfect example of the practice - a standard M1936 enlisted man's tunic which has been adapted by the addition of officer grade insignia. No modifications have been made to the actual design, although some officers went as far as having a more pointed collar and turn-back cuffs added.

An SS-rune collar patch is worn on the right side (the original Totenkopf units were redesignated SS Infantry Regiments in 1941); and the rank patch bears the three 'pips' and two doubled silver braids of SS-Hauptsturmführer. On the right sleeve is a machine-embroidered Skijäger qualification badge (see opposite); on the left, an enlisted grade sleeve eagle and the cuff title 'Nord'. The ribbon of the Iron Cross 2nd Class is displayed in the buttonhole; and on the right breast pocket, an embroidered cloth presentation of the Deutsches Kreuz (German Cross), an award which bridged the gap between the Iron Cross 1st Class and the Knight's Cross.

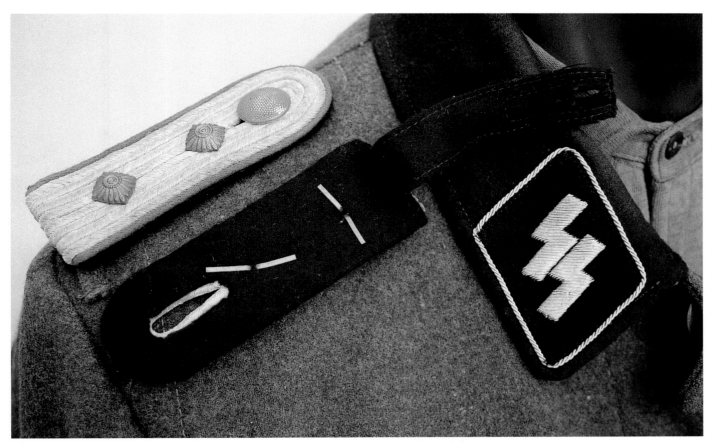

The SS-Division 'Nord' was assembled in Norway in June 1941 mainly from the internal security regiments Totenkopf-Standarten 6 & 7; it was designated as a mountain division in May 1942, and finally as 6th SS Mountain Division in October 1943. It fought mainly on the northern sector of the Eastern Front.

(Above) The slip-on shoulder straps are in the flat silver cord, with gilt rank 'pips', of subaltern officers. Note the *wiesengrün* underlay for Gebirgstruppe over the usual Waffen-SS black base; and the tongue of the slip-on strap, which fitted through a loop on the point of the shoulder.

(Upper right) This tunic is still fitted with the enlisted grade BeVo sleeve eagle rather than a more expensive officer's grade replacement. The 'Nord' cuff title is hand-embroidered (Handgestickt) in silver on a standard RZM cuff band, with seven-strand silver woven borders; this Latin or 'Antiqua' script was usual for such titles after

December 1939, replacing a Gothic 'Fraktur' script used for some earlier examples. This division was not officially awarded a cuff title, but photographs exist of them being worn; they are believed to be those of the Allgemeine-SS Oberabschnitt 'Nord', unofficially retained by transferred personnel.

(Lower right) The Skijäger military skiers' qualification badge; and the cloth version of the German Cross. Many officers preferred this to the full metal award for field wear, as it was lighter and less likely to snag on obstacles. Note the attachment stitching to both pieces.

Officer's service tunic, 'Totenkopf' Division

Waffen-SS officers, like their counterparts in other branches of the Wehrmacht, were responsible for procurement of their own uniforms and accessories, being provided with an allowance or coupons towards the cost. Officers usually required several uniforms, for parade and/or walking-out and for field service dress. This four-pocket tunic of M1936 pattern is an example of an early war quality piece in the Army, rather than the previous SS-Verfügungs-truppe style; note that the lower pockets are box-pleated patch rather than 'slash' pockets. Constructed from a fine quality tricot material, with a sharply pointed dark green collar and deep turn-back cuffs, it carries the insignia of an SS-Obersturmführer of the 'Totenkopf' Division.

The collar patches are particularly interesting, both bearing that forma-tion's death's-head insignia in a 'handed' or 'mirror image' pair facing inwards; seen in a number of early-war photographs, this later became a much rarer variation.

The first lieutenant's shoulder straps are con-ventional, with double white over black underlay and a single gilt 'pip'. On the upper left sleeve is a hand-worked silver bullion eagle. The officer grade cuff title on the lower left sleeve, bearing the death's-head emblem, is the type associated with SS-Totenkopf-Standarte 1 (later, SS-T-Infanterie-Regiment 1). In September 1942 all divisional person-nel were ordered to adopt the script 'Totenkopf' title, but veterans were later occasionally photo-graphed still wearing this pattern.

The 'Totenkopf' Division was formed in November 1939 from internal security regiments of the Totenkopfverbände (a separate organisation from the SS-Verfügungstruppe which formed the basis of the Waffen-SS), several of which had seen action in Poland. The 'SS-T-Division' served in the French campaign in 1940, but thereafter only in Russia. It was up-graded to Panzer-Grenadier (mechanised) status in November 1942, and became a Panzer division in summer 1943.

(Above) The pointed collar of fine dark green wool bears the rarely seen 'mirror image' variation of the 'Totenkopf' Division's special collar patches in fine bullion. These are also found with both death's-heads facing to the wearer's right; on some they are revolved so that top and bottom align with the short sides of the patch. However, most officers of the division wore a death's-head on their right patch and the usual rank insignia on their left. The woven tailor's label at the neck identifies W.Müller & Co. of Wien (Vienna).

(Upper right) The fine bullion sleeve eagle, and the cuff title, displaying the typically fine workmanship found on officers' grade insignia. These were hand-embroidered over cardboard blanks in order to maintain consistency of style. Note the cuff title's seven-strand silver wire border.

(Lower right) The plain silver-grey artificial satin (polished cotton) lining, with striped cotton in the sleeves. A second label inside the left internal pocket gives details of the owner, named as an SS-Obersturmführer Kuhn. Note the dagger hanger strap and clip under the left armpit.

Officer's service tunic, 'Prinz Eugen' Division

Made from a fine, ribbed grey twill and with four box-pleated patch pockets, this tunic has a collar faced with dark-green cloth which is tailored, pressed and badged for wearing open over a collared shirt and tie. Officers most often wore this style as walking-out dress, the tunic for field wear having the closing fall collar.

The left collar patch displays the rank of SS-Obersturmführer, balanced on the right collar by the special '*Odalrune*' of the 7.SS-Freiwilligen-Gebirgs-Division 'Prinz Eugen', both edged in officers' silver cord. The shoulder strap underlay is in the light green *(hellgrün)* of mountain rifles - apparently described as 'meadow-green' *(wiesengrün)* after March 1942. The divisional cuff title is a hand-embroidered specimen in heavy silver bullion, each of the letters being worked over a cardboard template *(Unterlagen)*; the very nature of this method means that a variety of examples will be encountered. Also shown on the upper right sleeve is the officer's pattern of the Edelweiss tradition badge worn by all SS mountain troops; this too is worked in heavy bullion, the enlisted ranks' pattern being in machine-embroidered cotton or wool. Above the hand-embroidered eagle on the upper left sleeve is the Narvik Shield campaign decoration.

The lining is made from a bottle-green brushed cotton. The inside left breast pocket carries a maker's label for 'F.Lehrmann, Suhl 1940'. There is a slot inside the lower left pocket for the hanger of a dress dagger.

The 7th SS Volunteer Mountain Division 'Prinz Eugen' was formed early in 1942 to harness the recruitment potential of the considerable ethnic German population in the Balkans and on the borders of the old Austro-Hungarian empire; most of the officers were Austrian or Rumanian. From late 1942 to late 1944 it was employed against Balkan partisans, and thereafter against the advancing Red Army as well.

(Above) **As a 'Germanic' but non-German formation, the division was not deemed eligible to wear the SS-runes; instead, all ranks wore on the right collar the Odalrune patch, here an example in fine bullion. The slip-on shoulder straps have the light green underlay of the Gebirgstruppe over the usual black base; note the underside, with a black wool tongue and the wire pins securing the single gilt rank 'pip' of SS-Obersturmführer. On the upper right sleeve is worn an officer's quality Edelweiss SS mountain troops' badge.**

(Upper right) **The Wehrmacht's 'Narvik' commemorative campaign shield is worn on the upper left sleeve on a field-grey backing sewn to the tunic, above a fine hand-worked bullion sleeve eagle. As no Waffen-SS units took part in this campaign, the wearer must presumably have been in spring 1940 a member of either the 2nd or 3rd Army Mountain Divisions who subsequently transferred to the Waffen-SS.**

(Lower right) **The hand-embroidered officer's cuff title in an unusual, heavily-woven block script.**

NCO's M1936 service tunic, 'Das Reich' Division

The tunic shown here is an M1936 pattern badged for an SS-Oberschar-führer of the 'Das Reich' Division. The M1936 tunic is easily distinguished by the box-pleated patch pockets with scalloped flaps, and the stand-and-fall collar faced in dark green. Tunics came from the factory with basic enlisted grade insignia machine-sewn in place. Those worn by senior NCOs had to have the Tresse collar braid fitted later, and varying degrees of sewing skill will be encountered; this process also involved moving the collar patches to accomodate the braid. This example has collar braid of wartime silver-grey type, while the detachable shoulder straps display the earlier 'pearl-white' braid. There was also a bright silver Tresse which was intended for parade tunics, but was sometimes seen on field service items. The sleeve eagle on this tunic is the NCO grade BeVo version. In the second buttonhole the ribbon for the War Merit Medal is displayed; since - unlike the War Merit Cross - this was a civilian award, it must date from before this soldier's enlistment.

This tunic is heavily stamped with Russian capture marks, but still bears the German stamps which are usually found on the outer edge of the inner right lining.

Second in seniority only to the 'Leibstandarte SS Adolf Hitler', the SS-Verfügungs-Division was raised in October 1939 around the three SS-VT regiments 'Deutschland', 'Germania' and 'Der Führer'. Retitled 'Reich', and then 'Das Reich' (May 1942), it was up-graded to a Panzer-Grenadier division that November and to 2.SS-Panzer-Division in January 1944. The division fought in the West in 1940, Yugoslavia in 1941, then in Russia from June 1941 to February 1944. After service in France and the Ardennes in 1944-45 it returned to the Eastern Front for the final months of the war.

(Above) **The shoulder straps are piped in the light grey Waffenfarbe which denotes a staff appointment; this senior NCO was clearly not working in the main SS central command departments in Berlin, since his tunic was captured in Russia. Notice the contrast between the two commonly encountered wartime qualities of Tresse: 'pearl-white' on the shoulder straps, and 'mouse-grey' on the collar. Note also the black fixing tongue on the shoulder straps. The NCO grade runic collar patch is worked in heavy bullion; the BeVo sleeve eagle, not illustrated here, is also of NCO quality.**

(Upper right) **The 'Das Reich' divisional title, on a standard RZM issue cuff band with seven strands of silver wire on each border. After September 1942 this was ordered into use by all personnel, replacing the regimental titles previously worn by members of the division's 'Deutschland', 'Germania' and 'Der Führer' regiments.**

(Lower right) **The maker is shown as 'Reitz', above the usual array of size measurements, and the depot stamp 'H39' (Hannover 1939).**

NCO's M1936 service tunic, 'Langemark' Division

This tunic, bearing the rank insignia of an SS-Hauptscharführer of Pioniere (assault engineers) in the Flemish 'Langemark' Division, is of M1936 pattern. Interestingly, the body has been retailored to increase the chest size and at the same time the four box-pleated patch pockets have also been replaced or repaired, showing a noticeable mismatch in colour. This was obviously an official repair performed at a depot; there are two different size stampings on the lining, one showing the new measurements.

The use on the right hand collar patch of the three-legged rotating swastika or 'Trifos' dates back to an original Flemish volunteer regiment ('Nordwest') in April 1941; individuals wore it for a time in the later Freiwilligen Legion Flandern. The SS-runes became standard, but both emblems seem to have been worn in the subsequent 6.SS-Freiw.-Sturmbrigade 'Langemark' of 1943-44, and in the 27.SS-Freiw.-Gren.-Div.'Langemark' raised around its survivors in autumn 1944.

The shoulder straps are conventional, with a black base and in this case, black Waffenfarbe piping for a Pioneer unit. Straps and collar are edged with the silver Tresse of senior NCO status. A BeVo-woven eagle is machine-sewn to the upper left sleeve, and on the lower left sleeve is the Flemish volunteers' national shield - a black rampant lion on golden yellow - and the 'Langemark' cuff title.

A Flemish volunteer battalion - the Freiwilligen Legion Flandern - went to the Leningrad front in November 1941. In May 1943 the Legion was expanded around the few survivors, new recruits, and the former SS-Totenkopf-Standarte 4 'Langemark' into the 6th SS Volunteer Assault Brigade 'Langemark'. In autumn 1944 an influx of Flemish collaborator refugees from now-liberated Belgium were conscripted in to expand the brigade, on paper, into the 27th SS Volunteer Grenadier Division 'Langemark'. These formations all served on the Russian Front only.

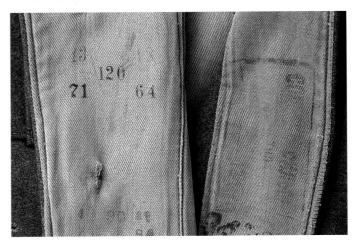

(Above) Wartime photographs show officers and men of the 'Langemark' brigade and division wearing the three-legged 'Trifos', although SS-runes seem to have been at least as common. The collar and shoulder straps are edged in silver senior NCOs' braid, and the Waffenfarbe is black for Pioneers.

(Upper right) The German-made version of the Flemish national shield, probably dating from 1944, is easily distinguished by the black surround; earlier Belgian-made shields lack this. The cuff title is a straight RZM issue piece, with seven-strand silver edging and silver-grey cotton lettering in Latin script; it has been machine sewn to the sleeve.

(Lower right) On the lining of standard grey ribbed twill the two different size markings can be seen; the chest size (the central number) has been enlarged from 90cm to 120cm and the arm length (lower right) shortened from 84cm to 64cm. The stamps on the right are post-capture Russian museum control marks.

NCO's M1940 service tunic

This is a classic example of a common Waffen-SS tunic. The most readily identifiable feature when distinguishing between an SS-Bekleidungswerke product and an Army-made tunic supplied to the W-SS is the number of holes provided for the belt supporting hooks: SS-manufactured tunics have two or occasionally four holes, while Army tunics – by far the more common – have three. This Army-made tunic is of the standard M1940 cut, with four pleated patch pockets, and the collar manufactured in the same cloth as the body; the green collar was discontinued to simplify production. It has the standard three belt hook eyelets. The insignia consist of a runic collar patch in NCO grade bullion (although most NCOs' tunics simply retain the enlisted mens' runes in silvery-grey cotton), with the two-'pip' ranking of SS-Oberscharführer. The sleeve eagle is also of NCO grade, being made of BeVo-woven metallic thread. The shoulder straps are piped in orange Waffenfarbe; this was used by the military police of the SS-Feldgendarmerie, by the recruiting and replacement branches, and by certain technical specialists. Both the collar and shoulder straps are faced with bullion wire Tresse. The lining carries many Russian 1943 capture stamps, and a Red Army Museum tag states that this tunic was taken from an 'underofficer' (NCO) of the 'LAH' ('Leibstandarte') in 1943. A cuff title has been removed, leaving a mark where it was machine-sewn in place. The collar is pressed open for wear with a shirt collar and tie.

Much discussion has taken place among collectors as to what constitutes a 'truly Waffen-SS tunic'. While the SS had their own clothing manufacturing facilities, known as the SS-Bekleidungswerke or SS-BW, this organisation struggled to keep up with the increasing demands of a rapidly expanding service. It is generally accepted that the SS-BW provided at most about 20 per cent of W-SS clothing requirements, the rest being drawn from Army production. This reliance on Army sources dated from the very beginning of the war, with the transition from the SS-VT earth-grey uniform to the field-grey combat uniform.

(Above) **The collar of this example shows clearly that the enlisted ranks' collar patches applied at manufacture have been replaced upon the wearer's promotion to senior NCO rank, and shifted to make room for the addition of Tresse edging braid. Note the bullion NCO quality runic patch.**

(Upper right) **This sleeve eagle is the NCO pattern in silver wire BeVo embroidery; it is attached to the sleeve by heavy machine sewing. Most NCOs' tunics simply retained the enlisted grade eagle with which they came from the factory.**

(Lower right) **The markings on the lining of grey ribbed drill material. On the left side are the standard German size stamps, with the manufacturer location above (Koblenz) and the issuing depot stamp 'M41' (Munich, 1941) below. The other stamps are Russian markings, the lower right series being the serial number given to the item on capture. The lower left stamp indicates that this piece was captured in 1943. The other stamps are museum control markings. Note the museum tag at the neck giving capture details.**

NCO's M1940 service tunic, 'Nordland' Division

This M1940 pattern tunic is badged for a Finnish volunteer SS-Oberscharführer of the 'Nordland' Division. It is of standard pattern, with four box-pleated pockets and a field-grey collar. The grey drill liner is marked with the sizes and the depot stamp 'St.41' (Stettin, 1941)'; on the wound dressing pocket there is also a stamp for a Stettin manufacturer. At the neck is a Red Army Museum tag stating that this is a trophy taken in the Northern Caucusus; the newly-formed 'Nordland' Division was engaged against partisans in autumn 1943, before transfer to the northern sector of the Eastern Front that November. The right collar patch displays the divisional symbol, a circular presentation of the swastika called the *'Sonnenrad'* or sun-wheel (probably the most ancient form of this symbol). The shoulder straps for SS-Oberscharführer are piped in deep Bordeaux red, the Waffenfarbe used by the W-SS legal service, but in this case far more likely to identify a rocket mortar (Nebelwerfer) unit, as it did in the Army. The shoulder straps also feature slides with a chain-stitched 'N' for 'Nordland', this being carried over from previous use in the 'Nordland' Regiment of the 'Wiking' Division. The sleeve eagle is a heavily machine-woven example, possibly Finnish-made and not of standard RZM manufacture. The cuff title is the issue RZM pattern for the 'Nordland' Division; above this is a Finnish national shield. This specimen is the RZM pattern, an earlier Finnish-made version being phased out with the change-over to the 'Nordland' Division from 'Wiking'.

The 11th SS Volunteer Panzer-Grenadier Division 'Nordland' was established in March 1943. The nucleus was the Scandinavian 'Nordland' Regiment (which had been part of the 'Wiking' Division), to which were added the former Danish Free Corps and Norwegian Volunteer Legion, and ethnic Germans from Hungary and Rumania. The division was heavily engaged on the Baltic front and in Pomerania in 1944-45, and survivors were among the last defenders of Berlin in April/May 1945.

(Above) **Despite their impeccably 'Aryan' status the division did not wear the SS-runes, but their own Teutonic sun-wheel emblem. Note the chain-stitched 'N' shoulder strap slide, worn briefly in 1943. Bordeaux red Waffenfarbe shoulder strap piping almost certainly identifies 'smoke' or rocket mortar troops (Nebelwerfertruppe).**

(Upper right) **The lining is of standard M1940 pattern in grey drill material. The German issue stamps appear on the inner right side, on both the upper edge and on the wound dressing pocket. Note the belt hook suspension tapes, used prior to the introduction of permanently fitted hook suspenders.**

(Lower right) **Left sleeve insignia. Foreign volunteers wore a national shield, usually on the lower left sleeve above the cuff title. Several nationalities had shields made in their native countries, but these were eventually replaced by German-made RZM patterns. This cuff title, and the national shield for Finnish volunteers - who served in about battalion strength with the 'Nordland' - are both standard RZM issue pieces. The sleeve eagle, however, appears to be constructed in the same way as the officer's bullion pattern but in light-grey cotton. This is thought to be a Finnish-made piece, probably purchased while the wearer was on home leave.**

NCO's M1940 service tunic, 'Westland' Regiment

A military police (Feldgendarmerie) troop or company formed part of each division's headquarters troops, tasked with enforcing military law, guarding supply routes and directing traffic. This senior NCO's tunic with Feldgendarmerie distinctions also bears regimental insignia of the Dutch volunteer 'Westland' Regiment within the 'Wiking' Division. This suggests a Dutch NCO with either previous experience as a police officer, or simply a particularly good record, detached from his infantry unit to the divisional military police element.

The lining of this regular M1940 pattern tunic is stamped with the sizes and the issuing depot mark 'M42' (Munich, 1942); this accords with the 'Westland' Regiment's known depot. The collar runes are of NCO grade bullion. The left patch and the shoulder straps display SS-Oberscharführer rank, and the latter have orange Waffenfarbe piping as well as 'W' cyphers for 'Westland'. This cypher was worn by enlisted ranks in chain-stitch on a black wool strap slide, and in stamped metal for senior NCOs and officers; this NCO has acquired - either through vanity or simple availability - the officer grade cyphers in gilt metal instead of the regulation silver NCOs' version. On the upper left sleeve is the Police pattern eagle, as also worn by Army Feldgendarmerie personnel; in the W-SS branch the standard SS national eagle was often worn in preference. Below this is the Netherlands volunteers' national shield, above the regimental cuff title.

The 10th SS Infantry Regiment 'Westland' was raised in 1941 as part of the 'Wiking' Division, from Dutch and Flemish-speaking Belgian volunteers. It was redesignated a Panzer-Grenadier regiment after November 1942. With the rest of the division, 'Westland' saw heavy fighting throughout the Russian campaign, particularly at Rostov in November 1941, in the Cherkassy Pocket in winter 1943/44, in Poland in 1944, and in Hungary at the end of that year.

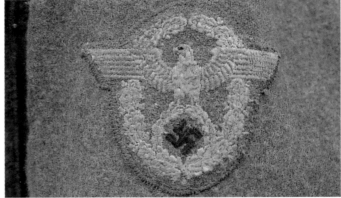

(Above) NCO's quality bullion runic collar patch; and orange-piped shoulder straps for SS-Oberscharführer of Feldgendarmerie. Note the ornate 'W' cypher for the 'Westland' Regiment; this is of gilt officer's pattern, instead of the regulation NCO grade silver finish.

(Upper right) The German Police sleeve eagle, officially worn by SS-Feldgendarmerie from late 1942 until late 1944, when it was replaced by the standard Waffen-SS national eagle - although many military policemen never wore the Police pattern at all.

(Lower right) Left forearm insignia. The 'Westland' title is the standard RZM pattern with Latin style lettering. The national shield for the Netherlands is also the German-made pattern, distinguished by its black border.

NCO's M1940 service tunic, 'Norge' Regiment

This tunic is of standard M1940 pattern; it bears the usual size stamps and is dated 1941. There are also numerous Russian capture stamps inside. The shoulder straps for the rank of SS-Ober-scharführer are piped in Jäger-green. They also show the curious use of what appear to be invert-ed number '7' cyphers, possibly to convey a com-pany number '2'; these are in stamped gilt and appear to have been pre-sent for a long time. On the upper left sleeve is an NCO grade national eagle. On the lower left sleeve are the Norwegian national shield in the RZM pattern; and the 'Norge' cuff title identify-ing SS-Pz-Gren-Regt 23 'Norge' (norwegisches Nr.1) within the 11.SS-Freiw-Pz-Gren-Div 'Nordland' from November 1943. (In March 1945 the first battalions of this unit and SS-Pz-Gren-Regt 24 'Danmark' were detached to serve under command of the 5.SS-Pz-Div 'Wiking' for the rest of the war.)

On the upper right sleeve is the qualification badge for ski troops (Skijäger), instituted in late 1944 and considered extremely rare. Its pres-ence, and the green Waffenfarbe on the shoul-der straps, may indicate that the wearer was a member of SS Ski Battalion 502 in early 1945, this unit being enti-tled to the 'Norge' cuff title. The sleeve badge was worn in conjunction with a stamped white metal cap badge showing a spray of oakleaves (iden-tical to the regular Jäger badge) with a single ski superimposed diagonally; this was worn on the left side of the M1943 Einheitsfeldmütze.

The first Norwegian contribution to the Waffen-SS was the Freiwilligen Legion Norwegen in 1941. This regiment served on the Eastern Front until mid-1943, when it was formally disbanded and its survivors were transferred to serve in the 'Nordland' Division, forming with men from the former 'Nordland' Regiment a new unit awarded the title 'Norge'.

(Above) **As a former member of the Freiwilligen Legion Norwegen this SS-Oberscharführer has retained the Legion's rampant lion right collar patch. This example is the first pattern in stamped metal (its silver finish now faded with age); the later pattern was machine-woven in grey thread, and some versions omitted the axe. This emblem was replaced by the SS-runes after the transfer to the 'Wiking' Division. Note also the Jäger-green Waffenfarbe, probably indicating that this man was a Skijäger; and the odd-looking cyphers, possibly added to a walking-out tunic to identify 2nd Company of the battalion.**

(Upper right) **The Skijäger badge on the upper right arm, instituted for qualifying troops in August 1944. This example is in machine-embroidered cotton; a BeVo machine-woven version was also issued.**

(Lower right) **Left forearm insignia. The regimental cuff title is in what is commonly termed 'BeVo-like' weave; note the flat weave of the edge stripes, as opposed to the ribbed weave of a true BeVo of Wuppertal piece. Again, the black edge of the Norwegian volunteers' national shield identifies the RZM-issue version.**

NCO's M1940 service tunic, 'Wiking' Division

This tunic belonged to a Finnish volunteer, one of some 400 in the ranks when the 'Wiking' Division took part in the invasion of the Soviet Union on 22 June 1941. It is a classic M1940 pattern, with four box-pleated patch pockets, five front buttons, and a collar in the same *feldgrau* cloth as the rest of the tunic. Insignia consists of the standard runic and rank collar patches, machine-woven sleeve eagle, and shoulder straps indicating the rank of SS-Unterscharführer and piped in the rose-pink Waffenfarbe of both armoured and anti-tank troops. Of most interest are the distinctive Finnish national shield and the cuff title on the lower left sleeve. The former is the German-made RZM issue BeVo machine-woven pattern, produced in response to a shortage of Finnish-made shields and also indicating a desire to standardise production of all foreign volunteer shields. The 'Wiking' cuff title was introduced in September 1942 in the RZM pattern shown here; a machine-woven pattern was also produced from 1943.

This tunic was manufactured by a Berlin company, and carries the depot stamp 'B II 40'; the 'B 40' stands for Berlin, 1940; the Roman numeral 'II' indicates the grade of wear *(Garnituren)* - 'I' being new and 'IV' the lowest grade, suitable only for fatigue wear.

The 'Wiking' Division was formed from December 1940, incorporating both German and foreign troops. Created around the 'Germania' Regiment from the 'Das Reich' Division, it was largely made up of volunteers from various 'Germanic' nations, occupied or friendly: Danes, Norwegians, the Flemings of the 'Westland' Regiment, some Swiss and Finns, and later ethnic Germans from the Balkans. The division - up-rated to a Panzer-Grenadier formation in November 1942, and to 5th SS Panzer Division in February 1944 - earned a high fighting reputation on the Eastern Front from 1941 to 1945.

(Above) The collar insignia and shoulder straps follow the standard patterns, with SS-Unterscharführer rank and the pink piping which in this case probably identifies an anti-tank unit. Note the enlisted quality grey SS-runes ('Wiking' was never designated as a foreign division; its title did not include the term 'Freiwilligen', and it wore the SS-runes from the start). See also the subdued collar Tresse, contrasting with the brighter braid on the detachable shoulder straps - a commonly seen feature.

(Upper right) The 'Wiking' cuff title and the distinctive Finnish national sleeve shield shown here are the RZM issue patterns. The shield was produced in response to a lack of Finnish-made examples; these had a more ornate machine-embroidered rampant lion on either a black, grey or red shield.

(Lower right) The markings stamped in the lining of the tunic inside the right front panel.

NCO's M1940 service tunic, 'Prinz Eugen' Division

This tunic demonstrates the kind of refurbished uniforms given to what the Germans regarded as 'second line' troops. It is a standard M1940 tunic, but it appears to have been refurbished at a depot, with all pockets being replaced and the body resized. Various tunics which had been reworked (or even foreign tunics which were suitable for adaptation) were issued to some of the foreign volunteer units. The insignia consist of the 'Prinz Eugen' Division's Odalrune collar symbol and a matching rank patch, and shoulder straps with SS-Unterscharführer rank and the mountain troops' meadow-green piping. The interesting sleeve eagle is actually the pre-war SS-VT model - another example of old stock being used up on second line uniforms? On the upper right sleeve *(see opposite)* is the Waffen-SS enlisted pattern Edelweiss tradition badge worn by all SS-Gebirgsjäger (mountain rifles) and their supporting divisional units. The RZM pattern 'Prinz Eugen' cuff title on the lower left sleeve was introduced in April 1942. It can be found with either seven-strand wire or white silk borders - the reason for the existence of these two almost identical versions is unknown. This title later also became available in a flat machine-woven version.

The 7th SS Volunteer Mountain Division 'Prinz Eugen' (see also note on page 51) was the first 'Volunteer' division of the Waffen-SS to be formed, and the first deemed unsuitable to wear the SS-runes collar patch; the German cadre who did qualify sometimes wore their runes as a left chest badge. After three years spent operating against the Yugoslavian partisans the division suffered heavy losses while fighting the Red Army, whose westwards advance threatened to cut off Army Group Lohr in the Balkans.

(Above) **The enlisted grade Odalrune collar insignia peculiar to the 'Prinz Eugen' Division; silver Tresse braid showing senior NCO status; and the meadow-green Waffenfarbe of the Gebirgsjäger.**

(Upper right) **The Edelweiss tradition badge was introduced for wear by Waffen-SS mountain troops in October 1943. This is the wool enlisted ranks' pattern; an example of the officers' bullion embroidered version is illustrated on page 51.**

(Lower right) **The sleeve eagle is of the pattern worn by the SS-Verfü-gungstruppe - forerunners of the Waffen-SS - before the war. It may indicate that this NCO was a pre-war SS-VT veteran who has retained it as a status symbol; or simply that old stocks were being used up for reasons of thrift when outfitting low priority units. The cuff title is the standard RZM pattern for enlisted ranks.**

Enlisted man's M1940 service tunic, 'Leibstandarte SS Adolf Hitler' Division

This typical Army-pattern M1940 tunic is identifid as such by its triple belt hook eyelets. The lining has size and manufacturer's markings, and the depot stamp 'E41' (Erfurt, 1941). Russian capture stamps inside state that it fell into Soviet hands in 1944. The collar patches display the typical wartime machine-embroidered runes on the right, and a black wool patch with the braid rank strip for SS-Sturmann on the left; they are machine-sewn to the tunic. The shoulder straps are piped in white, and display - in the same infantry Waffenfarbe - the 'LAH' unit cyphers on the slip-on wool loops introduced in 1940; previously the cyphers had been stitched directly into the body of the strap. (Security considerations, and the complexity of providing unit-specific shoulder straps during massive wartime troop transfers, brought about the change to removable strap insignia throughout the Wehrmacht.) Officers wore the same design but in stamped gilt metal, and senior NCOs in silver-coloured metal. On the left sleeve is the standard machine-embroidered sleeve eagle, sewn on with a zig-zag machine stitch; and a chevron displaying the rank of SS-Sturmann, this being hand-sewn by the recipient on promotion.

The most prominent piece of insignia is the 'Adolf Hitler' cuff title worn by all personnel of this premier SS formation; showing the signature of the Führer in Sütterlin script, it remained basically unchanged from 1933 until 1945.

The lineage of the Waffen-SS can be traced back to the establishment of the 'Leibstandarte SS Adolf Hitler' as the Führer's bodyguard in 1933. Expanded progressively from a battalion, to a motorised regiment, to a division, to a Panzer-Grenadier division, to the premier SS Panzer Division, and finally giving its name to a full Panzer corps, the 'LAH' was the élite of the élite throughout the war. Between 1939 and 1945 it fought in Poland, Holland and France, Yugoslavia, Greece, Russia, Italy, Normandy, the Ardennes, Hungary and Austria.

(Above) **The 'LAH' cypher embroidered from 1940 on removable slip-on loops was of slightly less elaborate design that that previously stitched directly on the shoulder straps. Note the slightly raised edges of the SS-runes; this is one of several variations.**

(Upper right & right) **The left sleeve insignia. Note the pattern inside the cuff band; the end of the maker's name 'BeVo-Wuppertal' on the turned-over end; and the line of** small dots along the reverse of the border. These are features of all genuine BeVo-made SS cuff titles; those which show dots and dashes instead of this line of identical dots must be considered reproductions.

Various patterns exist: RZM-manufactured, machine-woven, machine-embroidered, bullion-woven for officers and flat machine-woven for officers. The machine-woven example shown is the most common, introduced in 1943.

Enlisted man's M1940 service tunic, 'Theodor Eicke' Regiment

The tunic shown is a conventional SS-manufactured M1940 pattern for an enlisted man (note the two belt hook eyelets). The collar displays the enlisted pattern right hand symbol for the 'Totenkopf' Division, with a junior private's blank left patch. The shoulder straps are unremarkable, apart from the red piping identifying artillery. On the lower left sleeve is the regimental cuff title; it was only ever produced in this pattern, by BeVo of Wuppertal. The other interesting feature is the qualification badge for a Steuermann or boat coxswain. This badge was earned by those who completed courses in the use of motorboats and military pontoons. The badge is machine-embroidered in white cotton on a dark green badge cloth base and then hand-sewn to the lower left sleeve above any recipient's cuff title.

In March 1943, SS-Totenkopf-Infanterie-Regiment 3 (shortly afterwards redesignated SS-Pz-Gren-Regt 6) was granted the name and cuff title 'Theodor Eicke' in commemoration of the regiment's former commander, who was killed in action on the Eastern Front the previous month as commanding general of the 'Totenkopf' Division. Personnel continued to wear the division's death's-head right collar patch.

(Above) **The standard 'Totenkopf' Division enlisted grade collar patch and shoulder strap, the latter here piped in artillery red Waffenfarbe. Note the field-grey underside with black cloth reinforcement under the tongue.**

(Upper right) **This is the most frequently encountered pattern of machine-embroidered Waffen-SS enlisted grade sleeve eagle. Note the zig-zag machine stitching attaching it to the sleeve; hand-sewn examples may also be found.**

(Lower right) **The regimental cuff title awarded in March 1943, manufactured by BeVo of Wuppertal; and the interesting Steuermann qualification badge found on this tunic, in white on green badge cloth - note the hand stitching.**

Enlisted man's M1940 service tunic, 'Danmark' Regiment

This M1940 tunic for a senior private of SS-Pz-Gren-Regt 24 'Danmark' in the 'Nordland' Division is of entirely standard design. Its only remarkable feature is the rare set of insignia. The Danish national flag collar patch worn here was originally authorised in April 1942 for members of the Freikorps Danmark. It was presumably retained by an individual soldier as a sign of national pride; this unit was supposed to wear the 'sun-wheel' emblem of the 'Nordland' Division when the Freikorps Danmark survivors were incorporated into it in May 1943. (The roughly 40 per cent of Danes in the new regiment are known to have protested vigorously at the loss of their old unit's exclusively Danish identity, which would seem to support this odd survival.) The slip-on enlisted shoulder straps are piped in infantry and Panzer-Grenadier white Waffenfarbe. Below the standard machine-embroidered sleeve eagle is the cloth 'pip' insignia for the rank of senior private. The Danish volunteers' national arm shield was authorised in late 1941, and was worn haphazardly on the upper or lower left sleeve, or omitted altogether; this is a late, black-bordered RZM-issue example. The 'Danmark' cuff title was introduced with the creation of the regiment in summer 1943; it was made in only one version - this flat machine-woven weave which copies the basic appearance of the products of the BeVo company.

The Danish contribution to the Waffen-SS started as a volunteer regiment formed from June 1941 as the 'Freikorps Danmark' (an anachronistic title, mixing German and Danish spellings). The Freikorps fought alongside the 'Totenkopf' Division at the Demyansk Pocket in mid-1942, reportedly suffering 75 per cent killed and wounded. In May 1943 it was disbanded and its personnel passed into SS-Gren-Regt 1 'Danmark' within the new 'Nordland' Division. Later retitled SS-Pz-Gren-Regt 24 'Danmark'(dänisches Nr.1), the unit distinguished itself at Narva in Estonia and in Kurland (Latvia) in 1944-45; its first battalion was attached to the 'Wiking' Division in the last two months of the war.

(Above) **The extremely rare Freikorps Danmark collar patch displaying the Danish flag. The wearer apparently retained this insignia contrary to regulations; the 'Danmark' Regiment was supposed to wear the circular 'sun-wheel' of its parent 'Nordland' Division.**

(Upper right) **The single embroidered 'pip' on a black disc was the left sleeve rank insignia of SS-Oberschütze, SS-** Obergrenadier, etc. - senior private, the exact title depending upon the branch of service.

(Lower right) **The Danish volunteers' national shield was only sporadically available. Note the weave of the 'Danmark' cuff title, with its stippled lettering and simple border weave. This sought to mimic the appearance of those available from BeVo of Wuppertal.**

Enlisted man's M1940 service tunic, 'Nordland' Division

The tunic shown is for a Danish private of an anti-tank unit of the 'Nordland' Division. It is marked inside 'St.41', and was thus first issued from the Stettin depot in 1941. The lining is liberally marked with Russian stamps which show that it was captured by the Red Army in 1944. On the right collar is the 'Nordland' divisional 'sun-wheel' patch (however, all German staff and many transferred soldiers continued to wear the SS-runes collar patch). The enlisted grade shoulder straps are piped in rose-pink Waffenfarbe, which was worn by Panzerjäger as well as Panzertruppe. The sleeve eagle is the standard machine-embroidered type. On the lower left sleeve is the Danish national shield of the official RZM-manu-factured type. Below this is the 'Nordland' cuff title.

A note on the formation and service of the 11.SS-Freiw-Pz-Gren-Division 'Nordland' will be found on page 59 above.

(Above) The distinctive Sonnenrad right collar patch of the 'Nordland' Division, and enlisted ranks' shoulder straps piped in rose-pink; note the rayon reinforcing strip under the tongue.

(Upper right) The RZM pattern Danish volunteers' national shield; and a 'Nordland' cuff title, shown here in its early RZM pattern. This version was created in 1940 for the 'Nordland' Regiment of the 'Wiking' Division, which in 1943 provided cadre and personnel for the new 'Norge' Regiment of the 'Nordland' Division. In late 1943 a machine-woven version was produced by BeVo.

(Lower right) The lining displays both German and Russian markings. The German issue date and size measurements are seen on the lower left side. The garment's Russian capture number is stamped in dark blue, with a further catalogue number dating its capture to 1944.

Enlisted man's M1940 service tunic, 19th (Latvian) Division

The tunic shown is for a Latvian enlisted soldier of a reconnaissance unit. Of basic M1940 pattern, it displays on the right collar the 19th Division's distinctive emblem of a large swastika - in Latvian, the 'fire cross' - which was introduced in March 1943. The enlisted grade shoulder straps are piped in golden yellow denoting Aufklärungstruppe (reconnaissance troops). On the left arm is the enlisted sleeve eagle, this time in the later BeVo-manufactured machine-woven pattern. Below this is the German-made Latvian national shield; the version shown is the last of several patterns manufactured, the previous designs being variously handmade, screen-printed or machine-embroidered. Finally, this tunic carries the 'Kurland' cuff title, awarded as a battle honour in March 1945 and locally produced and issued inside the cut-off Courland peninsula of western Latvia.

In February/March 1944 the 19.Waffen-Grenadier-Division der SS (lettische Nr.2) was formed – while its constituent units were actually locked in battle – from the reinforced remains of a Latvian volunteer brigade. These troops continued to distinguish themselves in fierce fighting along the Baltic coast to defend their country from the advancing Russians, and particularly in October 1944/April 1945 in Courland.

(Above) The distinctive 'fire cross' collar insignia introduced in March 1943 for the 19. was also worn by the Latvian 15.Waffen-Grenadier-Division der SS (lettische Nr.1) from March 1943 until autumn 1944, when they were awarded their own distinctive 'sun and stars' collar patch. The regulation black enlisted grade shoulder straps are piped in the golden yellow of reconnaissance troops, formerly the Waffenfarbe of the cavalry branch.

(Upper right) The BeVo machine-woven sleeve eagle, most often observed in use late in the war; it was manufactured in silver-grey but after the passage of time a 'bronze' tarnish is normal. The Latvian national shield illustrated is the last of several patterns produced. Note the machine stitching to both pieces.

(Lower right) The 'Kurland' cuff title was produced at the weaving mill at Kuldiga, and because of shortages various base materials were used; at least three distinctive appearances were observed using e.g. cotton sheet and heavier twill – but the basic design remained unchanged. The example shown is one of the more commonly encountered types.

NCO's M1944 service tunic

For reasons of economy several changes were made to the service tunic during the war years, such as omitting the pocket pleats. In 1944, however, a new service uniform was introduced which departed completely from previous designs. The Model 1944 tunic was apparently a copy of the British battledress blouse. The illustrated example was produced by the SS-Bekleidungswerke clothing factories. It has a wide, open collar, two inner and two outer chest pockets, and a broad waist band; there are six front buttons, and the *Armelschlitz* or slash openings at the wrist are eliminated.

(Above) The lining is of a gunmetal-grey herringbone twill material, which seems to be characteristic of SS - rather than Army - manufactured M1944 blouses. Several mismatched pieces of lining material are visible, emphasising the inferior 'utility' construction methods in the exhausted Reich. The jacket has two internal chest pockets, fastened by pressed paper buttons. There are no provisions for belt support hooks at the waist.

(Left) There is a stamped group of size measurements on the inner left side, and the 'SS-BW' stamp indicating SS manufacture on the right side.

(Above) The tunic bears the last patterns of collar patch and shoulder strap. The SS-rune patch is now BeVo machine-woven, flat on a smooth cotton base, not embroidered on wool as before. The shoulder straps eliminate the wool backing, leaving the raw edges of the Waffenfarbe piping exposed; and note also the simplified reinforced attachment tongue. The Tresse strips across the ends of this SS-Hauptscharführer's straps have been added by the company tailor to an SS-Unterscharführer's straps to make up - with the addition of two 'pips' - the correct rank. Not illustrated here is the sleeve eagle on this tunic, which is of the earlier machine-embroidered wool type seen in several other examples throughout this book, e.g page 71.

(Opposite) An untrained soldier could apply to become an officer trainee if he met National Socialist criteria. He was initially termed a *Führer-bewerber* or officer aspirant. After four months' basic training he became an *SS-Junker* (officer candidate) equivalent in rank to SS-Unterscharführer. During the subsequent six months' officer training course he progressed through several NCO ranks. A successful *Standarten-oberjunker* (graduate cadet) then served with a unit for a minimum of two months before

receiving the rank of SS-Untersturmführer.
    This M1944 blouse bears the insignia of a *Führerbewerber* of the 7th Volunteer Mountain Division 'Prinz Eugen' (see notes on pages 51 and 67). It is made from a very coarse grey reconstituted wool, economical to produce but providing poor protection and insulation. This is an Army-made example, differing little from SS-BW equivalents; it retains belt support hooks on internal hangers, and is lined with a grey rayon rather than herringbone twill. There are two internal patch pockets, and

markings showing size and date (1944) are stamped inside the upper left chest. The jacket displays the collar insignia and cuff title of the 'Prinz Eugen' division; a machine-embroidered enlisted sleeve eagle; and on the upper right sleeve the Edelweiss mountain troops' tradition badge.

(Detail) The standard RZM-manufactured cuff title introduced in 1942; it was first produced in this machine-embroidered style, and later in a flat machine-woven version.

Officer aspirant's M1944 service tunic, 'Prinz Eugen' Division

(Right) The Odalrune divisional collar insignia, and late war economy shoulder straps, unlined underneath to simplify construction. Note the meadow-green mountain troops' piping; and the double bars of 9mm Tresse for Führerbewerber (officer candidate). A single bar identified an Unterführeranwärter (NCO candidate).

(Below) The grey rayon lining is typical of an Army-manufactured item, and has belt hook suspenders under the armpits. Note the two internal pockets closed with grey glass buttons, and the markings on the upper left breast.

M1944 trousers

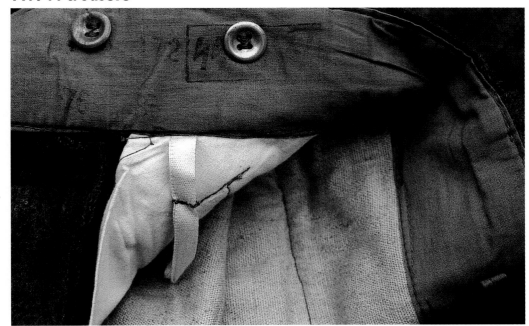

(Left) The waistband shows the size measurements, and the large 'SSBW' stamp of the SS-Bekleidungswerke. It is interesting to note that the trousers were stamped before the metal dish buttons were sewn on; such anomalies in production are common with very late items.

With the introduction of the Model 1944 tunic a new style of trousers was also issued. The M1944 trousers were more practical and easier to produce than the previous Keilhose. The legs were no longer of bloused design, but cut straight, with a simple tape and button tab to blouse the bottoms inside the web anklets now issued for use with ankle boots. The pockets now had buttoning flaps cut with a straight edge, and a small fob pocket at the front right side. The most significant change was that instead of being held up by braces (suspenders) the trousers now had belt loops fitted around the waist. This allowed the wearer to take down his trousers to answer a 'call of nature' without removing his belt equipment or tunic. Some trousers were issued with a herringbone twill cloth belt fitted with a three-prong buckle, very similar to the tropical trouser belt but marginally wider. The SS production trousers illustrated here utilise several different materials for linings and pockets.

Assault artillery NCO's tunic, 'Der Führer' Regiment

The short-waisted, double-breasted tunic issued to W-SS armoured vehicle crews was similar to the Army pattern - the differences were purely cosmetic. The points of the collar were of a more rounded cut; and the edge of the left front panel was cut to a vertical line rather than the outward slant of the Army jacket. The rear was a single panel, where Army tunics show a central seam. This example is made from *feldgrau* wool with a dark grey rayon lining; those for tank crews were cut identically but from black wool and usually with a black lining.

The front has four large grey glass buttons hidden by a fly; above are three smaller buttons, used to close the lapels up to the neck in cold weather - a hook-and-eye at the collar served the same purpose. The lining has a crescent-shaped patch pocket on the left, and a square-cut one on the right; hangers for belt hooks are also provided. Inside each hip is a 'tunnel' with cloth adjustment tapes. The cuffs have adjustable vents with two grey glass buttons.

Insignia are identical to those worn on the service tunic (unlike the Army, the W-SS did not provide special collar badges for armoured units). Distinctive unit insignia consist of metal 'DF' shoulder strap cyphers and the cuff title.

(Detail) The 'Der Führer' title is of RZM pattern in Latin script, with its unique quote marks, introduced in late 1939; this replaced a previous RZM pattern in Gothic script, without quotes. In 1943 a BeVo enlisted pattern also became available.

(*Above*) Insignia on Waffen-SS armoured vehicle uniforms were the same as on the service tunic. The only exception was that NCOs like this SS-Oberscharführer did not wear silver Tresse collar edging (although this was allowed briefly in the 'LAH' only). Note the red artillery Waffenfarbe; and officer grade stamped gilt metal 'DF' regimental cyphers being worn here by an NCO - such items were often in short supply, and whatever was available was acceptable on field uniforms.

(*Right*) The front of the armoured vehicle uniform is closed by four (occasionally, three) large buttons, behind a vertical fly front. Note two of the three smaller buttons high on the right panel for closing the lapels to the neck, and the two small buttons on the inside edge engaging loops inside the left panel.

CAMOUFLAGE UNIFORMS

M1940 camouflage smock

The greatest innovation in clothing introduced by the Waffen-SS was the mass production, and general issue in combat units, of camouflage clothing. The camouflage jacket (Tarnjacke) was a loose-fitting reversible over-smock made from a high-quality water-repellent cotton duck material, one side usually being screen-printed in a spring/summer colour scheme and the reverse showing autumn/winter colours. It was supposed to be worn over the wool service uniform and the field equipment; two large 'slash' openings each side of the torso were intended to allow the soldier to reach inside to get at his ammunition pouches. The troops soon abandoned this concept in practice, and wore their belt kit over the top of the smock for ease of access.

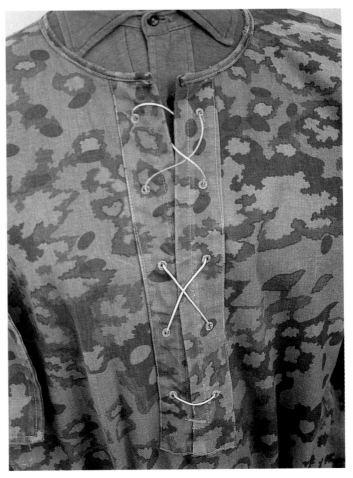

(Opposite) The Model 1940 smock shown here - with its spring/summer side exposed - replaced the first pattern, the M1938. That earlier model differed from the illustrated example only in having an elasticised neck opening, and a fly cover over the laced front opening on the autumn/winter side of the garment. The smock had a lace-up front opening extending down to the waist; loosely cut bellows sleeves; and two vertical openings at the chest with covering flaps. The waist and wrists were elasticised for a closer fit. At the ends of the sleeves cuffs of extra material extended to cover the hands, but in practice these were often tucked inside the elasticated wrists, or removed altogether. The pattern of camouflage shown here is referred to by collectors as 'Oakleaf A'.

(Above) Equipment access opening in the side of the torso of the M1938 and M1940 smocks. Note the shape of the flap, and the reverse camouflage scheme on the inside.

(Above right) The smock reversed to expose the autumn/winter side, printed in a scheme of browns and ochres.

(Right) The front opening, closed by laced eyelets. Note the reinforced panels, and the thread-edged eyelets. The lace shown is not as per issue, but is some kind of period replacement.

M1942 camouflage smock, Type 1

The smock shown is printed in the pattern referred to as 'Oakleaf B'. Between 1936 and 1945 there were approximately eight basic patterns of camouflage, with several oddities encountered as a result of manufacturing variations. As on the camouflage helmet covers (pages 32-37), the 'temperate' or spring/summer side is always dominant over the autumn/winter side, and so should be visible at the neck opening and hems when the smock is turned autumn side out.

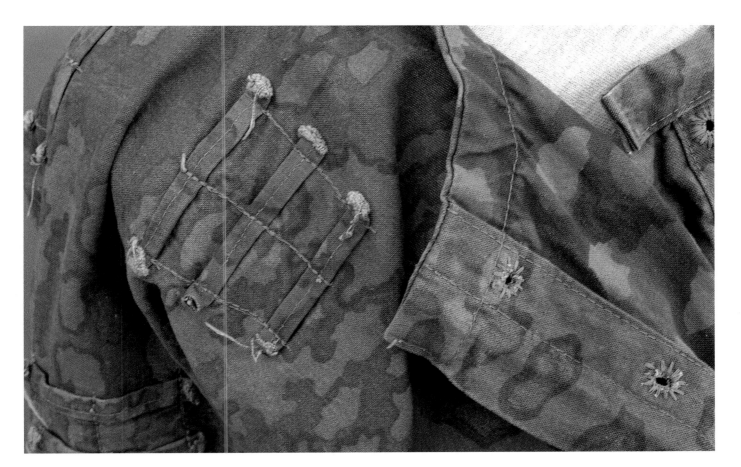

The later model of camouflage smock introduced improvements arising out of combat experience in the field. As the smock was no longer worn over the belt equipment the slash openings were eliminated from the chest; simultaneously two large pockets were introduced in the skirt. The 'bags' of these pockets were made of durable herringbone twill material, usually in a blue-grey colour; they could be simply pulled through the openings in the camouflage material depending upon which side of the smock was in use. Slightly scalloped buttoning pocket flaps were also provided on each side. Another addition were strips of material sewn in horizontal rows of three on the upper sleeves and front and back of the shoulders; these loops allowed the attachment of extra foliage for local camouflage.

The Type 2 M1942 smock was identical except that it had slightly angled pocket openings for better access.

(Above) The foliage loops were machine-sewn on in three horizontal rows of diminishing length, the top row being the widest. There were six sets of loops on the smock, one on each upper sleeve and one on both the front and back of each shoulder. Note also the hand-sewing of the chest lace holes on this example; others have machine-sewn reinforcing.

(Right) The blue-grey HBT pockets, turned through to the side in use; both sides had buttoning scallop-shaped pocket flaps. Note again the dominance of the temperate season camouflage side over the autumn/winter side, as seen at the neck opening.

M1944 camouflage uniform

In early 1944 the Waffen-SS introduced a new camouflage outfit which instead of being an accessory was a uniform in its own right. The jacket was cut almost identically to the M1943 pattern field tunic. It had four unpleated patch pockets, a fall collar that could be buttoned to the throat, adjustable cuff vents, and belt hook suspenders with two holes. It was a single-sided, non-reversible suit, intended to be used either on its own or as an overgarment in cooler weather. It proved to be very popular.

The tunic shown here is a later example made from a strong herringbone twill, printed on one side with the 'Dot' camouflage scheme developed in 1943. (Early examples of tunics and trousers were made of material left over from smock production, so a limited number will be found in the earlier reversible cotton duck, printed with patterns such as 'Oakleaf A' and 'B'.) Early uniforms were manufactured with a sleeve eagle, and also provided loops for shoulder straps, but this was an error: orders already forbade the use of anything other that the special sleeve rank insignia, in a system of green and golden yellow, which was produced for all garments worn without shoulder straps. Nevertheless, wartime photographs show examples of the use of all insignia, even including cuff titles, on this uniform.

It should also be noted that an almost identical tunic was produced for Police combat troops. It differed in that its top pockets had pleats; the belt hooks had three access holes; and the buttons were removable, secured with 'S'-shaped split pins.

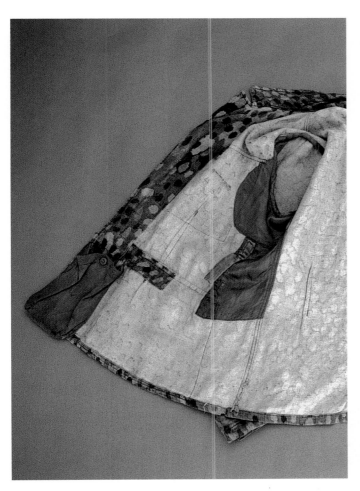

(Above) The interior of the M1944 tunic has almost no lining; there are simple strips of rayon material under the arms, and as belt hook suspenders. Note the single-side printing of the material, the double belt support hook holes, and the medical dressing pocket inside the right front.

(Above right) Regulations requiring subdued rank insignia to be worn on camouflage uniforms were often ignored. However, this tunic carries a BeVo machine-woven subdued sleeve eagle in a light tan, machine-sewn to the sleeve and thus possibly applied at the clothing factory; the similar chevron for SS-Sturmann is sewn on by hand.

(Right) The trousers of the M1944 uniform were initially cut in the M1937

service style, with straight legs, rear waist adjustment tab, suspender (braces) buttons, and three simple slash pockets. The pair illustrated here are the later and more common type, of herringbone twill and cut like the M1942 Keilhose. They have tapered legs with tightening tapes for blousing into web anklets, adjustment tabs at each hip, belt loops front and back, and a reinforcing patch over the seat area. There is a buttoning slash pocket at each hip, one on the right rear, and a small fob pocket at right front. Note the green drill lining, and the use of both brown bakelite and sand-painted metal buttons.

Camouflage winter parka

In the winter of 1942 the Waffen-SS issued troops with a winter clothing set which was basically the same as that used by the Army. It consisted of a padded parka and overtrousers made in field-grey on one side and snow white on the other. In 1943, however, the Waffen-SS were issued with new winter clothing which was reversible from SS pattern camouflage to white.

The parka was a protective hooded jacket, made with a layer of wool-rayon fibre sandwiched between white and camouflaged outer shell layers; it was produced in three sizes. The jacket had slanting pockets with buttoning flaps at each hip, adjustment strings for a tight seal at the bottom hem and around the hood, and adjustment tapes at the cuffs and waist (the waist tape was initially produced in camouflage on one side and white on the other, but later a simple grey canvas was used). The jacket's front closure was made to exclude drafts, with a fly flap buttoned from right to left to cover the main left-to-right fastening. The entire garment was reversible, with all adjustment tapes (waist and sleeves) being pulled through small slits, and pockets which could be accessed from either side. Usually standard stipple-finished metal buttons where used, with those on the winter side painted white, but some early jackets used large white pressed-paper buttons on the 'snow' side. Most encountered examples are in 'Oakleaf' and 'Blurred Edge' schemes, but some 'Dot' pattern parkas were also made; the parka illustrated here is in 'Oakleaf A' pattern.

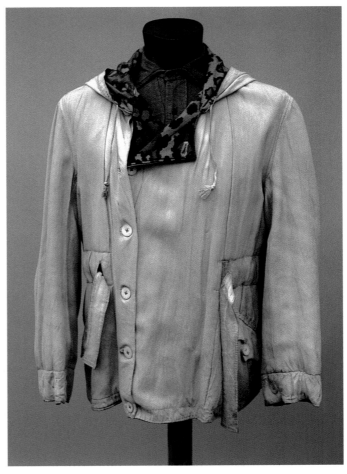

(Above) The front closure, intended to make a wind-proof seal; both sides have a fly which buttons across the opening. Note also the use of white pressed-paper buttons on the winter side and standard metal buttons on the temperate side.

(Above right) The hood was generously cut in order to fit over the steel helmet. Although this early parka is cut from 'Oakleaf A' spring/summer camouflage, most subsequent examples were made showing the autumn colours, which were more practical in the colder weather when these garments were issued.

(Right) The white-coloured snow camouflage side of the parka was identical to the camouflaged side. Note how the adjustment tapes at the waist are pulled through access slits for use on this side of the garment, and also the use of the contra-buttoning fly flap over the front closure.

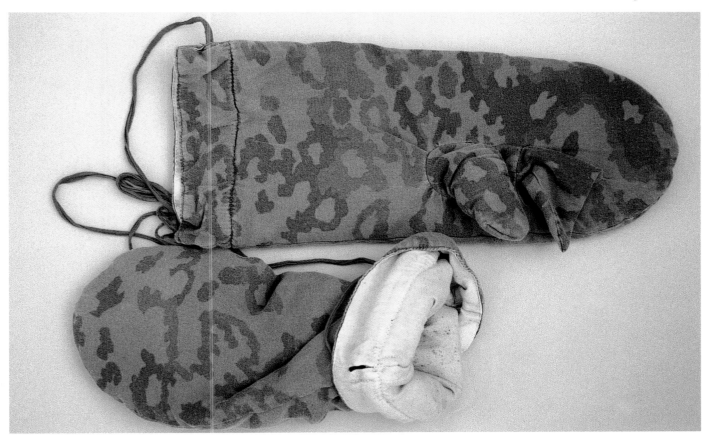

(Opposite) The straight-legged winter over-trousers were made in the same materials as the parka, cut in three sizes. There was an adjustment tape at the top rear and vents with tapes at the cuffs. Pockets at each hip had buttoned, square-cut flaps. The fly was cut at an angle to increase wind-proofing. Later examples had an additional wedge-shaped fly flap to increase this protection, and also reinforcement patches on the knees. The trousers were provided with cloth suspenders (braces).

(Above) Several acces-sories were available to complete the outfit. Padded mittens were pro-duced for both the grey-to-white and camouflage-to-white reversible uni-forms; the latter came in matching fabrics such as 'Oakleaf' and later 'Dot' pattern. The reversible mittens had long gauntlets and separated thumbs, and were joined by a long neck tape. Separate trigger fingers were later added, negating the need for special win-ter triggers on weapons.

A hood or 'toque' was also manufactured, basi-cally a close-fitting cloth helmet, which could be buttoned around the chin and had a wide neck guard to fit inside the parka collar.

(Right) A non-regulation hood produced for Norwegian SS ski troops - a good example of the many items locally modi-fied or manufactured by individuals or units to meet needs not covered by issue garments. (Other examples include camou-flage versions of service tunics, and variously modified smocks.) This hood is cut large enough to wear over a cap, and buttons across the chin. The outer is made from waterproofed 'Oakleaf A' material, lined with a black animal fur.

Early pattern camouflage Panzer tunic

Waffen-SS armour crews were originally issued with protective one-piece overalls in two versions: a winter weight, reversible from field-grey to white, and a summer weight produced in reversible camouflage colours. Both appeared early in 1943; and, like all one-piece combat clothing, they proved inconvenient (for one thing, a 'call of nature' required them to be taken off down to the knees). Around the beginning of 1944 a camouflage version of the two-piece wool armoured vehicle uniform was introduced. This was an almost exact copy of the popular reed-green herringbone twill fatigue uniform which had been introduced in 1941 for Army armoured reconnaissance crews, and subsequently 'acquired' by many Panzer troops.

The tunic shown is an early production example in 'Oakleaf' pattern camouflage. It is cut almost identically to the wool Panzer tunic, but omits the lining and the sleeve cuff vents; there is one simple patch pocket inside the left breast, and horizontal adjustment tapes are provided around the inside of each hip. While it has no sleeve eagle, it is provided with loops for the attachment of slip-on shoulder straps.

It is interesting that these early production examples made from remaining stocks of 'Oakleaf' and 'Blurred Edge' material include many made from mis-matched patterns used together. It seems that almost all tunics and trousers were made with the autumn side outwards, and while the material is printed on both sides these uniforms are not reversible.

(Above) While the cut of
the jacket is virtually
identical to that of the
wool armoured vehicle
uniform, it almost com-
pletely omits the lining.
Only a single patch pocket
is provided on the left
side. Note also the tapes
passing through 'tunnels'
at the waist, to allow for
adjustment to a better fit.
This interior view shows
an example of the sort of
mismatched patterns
encountered on many
early garments using
remnant stocks of materi-
al left over from smock or
Zeltbahn (tent section)
production. The left hand
temperate camouflage
panel, crossed by the tunnel for the black adjust-
ment tape, is made from
'Oakleaf B' scheme, while
that on the right of it in
the centre of the jacket is
'Oakleaf A'.

(Right) As on the wool
uniform, the front of the
jacket closes with four
large bakelite buttons
behind a fly front; the
smaller buttons above
this allow the lapels to be
fastened across up to the
neck for better protection
from the elements. Note
also the two buttoning
tabs to stop the inner flap
shifting. The shoulder
straps from the wool uni-
form are of conventional
enlisted ranks' type, in
black with pink Panzer
Waffenfarbe piping.

(Opposite) The jacket
being worn with trousers
cut from Italian camou-
flage material, which was
occasionally used by
members of the 'LAH'
and 'Hitlerjugend' divi-
sions after the former's
service in Italy.

Second pattern camouflage Panzer tunic

The introduction of 'Dot' pattern in 1944 superseded all other camouflage schemes; like the four-pocket M1944 service uniform, the camouflage Panzer uniform was now manufactured in this pattern. The material used was a distinctive herringbone twill, with an increasingly high artificial thread content. While this material was inherently strong it had poor insulation qualities, was heavy when wet and hard to dry. The material was printed on one side only, the reverse being a natural light brown or off-white.

The example illustrated here was obtained directly from an Estonian Waffen-SS veteran, who had been issued with it in 1945 just weeks before the end of the war. Special attention should be paid to the stitching on the underside of the collar. Instead of the usual zig-zag reinforcing stitch found on the service tunics, these jackets have a 'wavy line' which runs gently from one side of the collar to the other. Any examples of this pattern of jacket with zig-zag stitching should be regarded with suspicion, unless privately tailored.

All but the earliest examples of this uniform omitted the shoulder strap fittings, these being forbidden, as were any other insignia apart from the special subdued sleeve rank insignia in the system of green- and yellow-on-black bars and oak-leaves. Like many soldiers, however, this man ignored the regulation and has hand-sewn a BeVo eagle to his left sleeve.

(*Left*) The distinctive 'wavy line' stitching under the collar which is unique to this pattern of tunic - any examples which do not show this feature should be regarded with suspicion. Note the pattern of the HBT material.

(*Below left*) The front closure is by the same arrangement of buttons - these examples being of vulcanised rubber - as the wool vehicle tunic.

(*Below*) The jacket is virtually unlined, and has a single patch pocket inside the left chest. The colour of this reverse side of the printed material can vary from the bone colour seen here to a mustard brown.

Camouflage Panzer trousers

Matching trousers were issued with the camouflage Panzer tunic. Early examples appeared in 'Oakleaf' and 'Blurred Edge' patterns, later superceded by 'Dot' pattern herringbone twill. The cut resembled that of the Army Panzer wool trousers more closely than the Waffen-SS version. They were fitted with an internal waist belt of either camouflage material or HBT cloth. Hip pockets on each side were closed with slightly pointed single-button flaps rather than the square-cut two-button flaps found on SS wool Panzer trousers. There was also a small fob pocket at the right front, with a tab above it for securing the watch chain. There were no rear pockets. The legs were of a generous bloused cut for wear with ankle boots, and had vents at the bottom which closed with a tape and a single button.

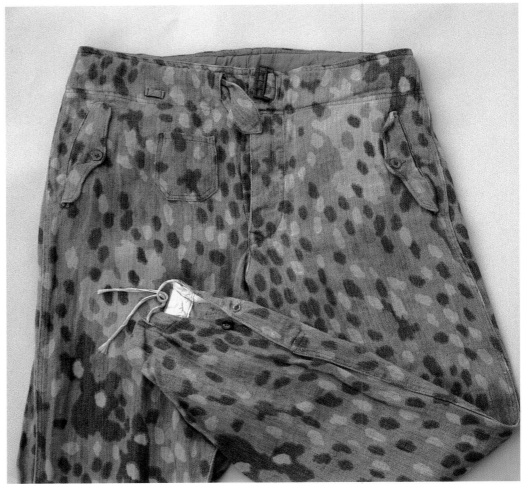

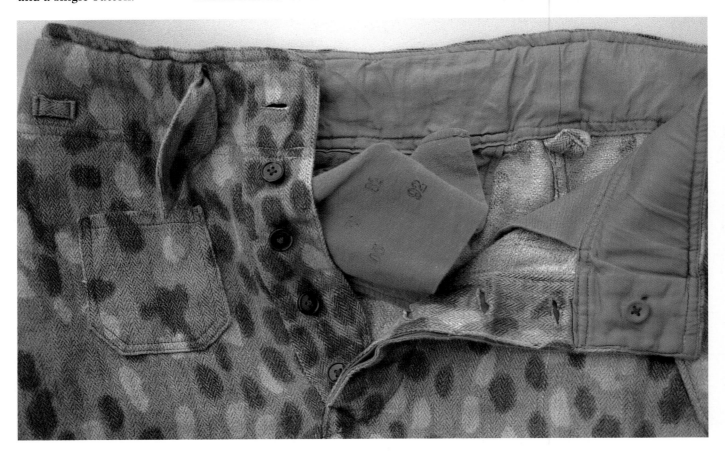

WAFFEN-SS INSIGNIA

Apart from the basic design of shoulder straps and sleeve rank badges, the insignia worn by the Waffen-SS were unique among the armed services. Rank titles and collar insignia reflected the paramilitary origins of the organisation. Rank was displayed both on the shoulders (or the left sleeve, by the senior privates and junior NCOs), and on the left hand collar patch. These collar patches were in the form of black cloth parallelograms. For all officer ranks they were edged with silver-coloured cord.

The collar patches for *(above)* SS-Brigadeführer (major-general) and *(below)* SS-Standartenführer. There were slight variations to general officers' collar designs during the war, but those shown date from the period 1942-45. All colonels' and general officers' insignia were in 'mirrored' pairs.

Officers' right hand collar patches showed the SS-runes *(Sigrunen, Doppelrunen)* in silver-coloured bullion. The embroidery was generally executed by hand over a cardboard template.

Members of the 3.SS-Panzer-Division 'Totenkopf' were required to wear the death's-head (Totenkopf) insignia instead of the SS-runes - a tradition carried over from the internal security and camp guard units of the Totenkopfverbände from which the division was formed. Enlisted ranks' death's-heads were machine-woven initially *(upper left)* in off-white, and later *(upper right)* in grey thread. *(Lower left)* A BeVo machine-embroidered pattern was produced from 1943. *(Lower right)* Officers' collar patches were hand-embroidered and edged with bullion cord. Several variations exist, including 'mirror image' patches, and death's-heads facing away from the centre; others were set vertically on the patch with the top and bottom parallel to its short edges. Early in the war officers and other ranks alike could be seen wearing pairs of death's-heads.

Below the rank of SS-Standartenführer (full colonel), the wearer's right hand patch displayed either the SS-runes or a distinctive unit insignia; and the left hand patch the rank, by a system of white metal 'pips' and silver braid strips. The very few exceptions to this general rule were provided by distinctive pairs of 'mirror image' unit insignia, particularly in Totenkopf units. From full colonel upwards, both patches displayed the rank insignia, which employed a system of embroidered silver-coloured oakleaves and white metal 'pips'. (See also translations of ranks on page 9.)

Throughout pages 103-109 we show on the right hand page the reverse, and thus the construction details, of the patches opposite.

In the case of senior officers the base material was black velvet over a buckram backing with silver-coloured (aluminium) bullion embroidery and cord edging.

Note the different buckram backings and the RZM issue tag.

Collar patches

The enlisted grade collar patches displayed the SS-runes and were not edged. They generally showed the runes in a cream or off-white colour. Various styles and angles exist, due to variations between manufacturers. The silver-coloured bullion example *(upper right)* is a style favoured by many NCOs. The patch *(lower right)* with the number '1' is for an enlisted member of the SS-Standarte Nr.1 'Deutschland'.

Later in the war the enlisted ranks' collar patches were made available in BeVo-manufactured machine embroidery. This produces a set of runes that are very flat and have a distinctive inner border around the edges of each rune. The silver-coloured embroidered patch *(upper left)* is for NCO grades. Below is a raw, unfinished NCO bullion-embroidered patch.

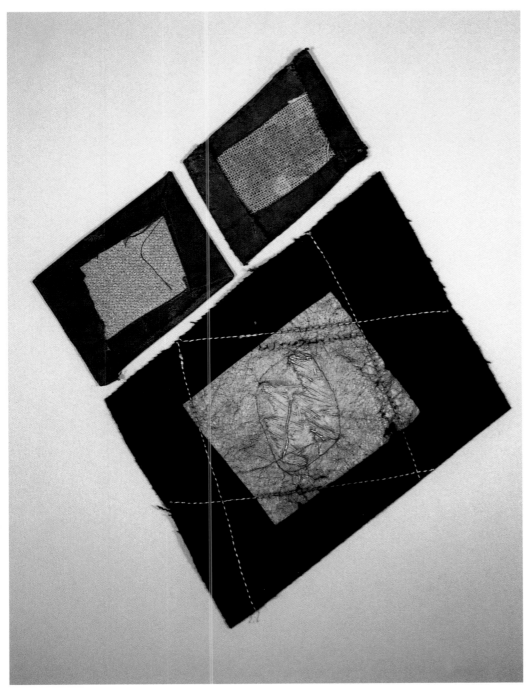

Collar patches

(Right & opposite) A selection of left hand rank patches of both officers and enlisted personnel. Note the variations in the white metal 'pips' used, which can vary slightly according to manufacturer. The doubled braid strip *(left centre)* is the type used in both officers' and enlisted mens' collar ranking; for some ranks two strips were used, closely butted, giving the appearance of four narrow lines.

(Top to bottom, left)
SS-Sturmbanführer;
SS-Obersturmführer;
SS-Untersturmführer.

(Top right)
SS-Unterscharführer

(Bottom right) SS-Mann.

(Right & opposite) **Foreign volunteer units of non-Germanic origin which were not entitled to wear the SS-runes were awarded various distinctive alternative insignia. Officer grade variants were available for most such units.**

(Top) **Two pairs of patches for officers of the Dutch 23.SS-Freiw-Pz-Gren-Div 'Nederland', using a runic symbol called a 'Wolfsangel'; both vertical and horizontal forms were observed.**

(Lower left) **Pair for an officer in the 'Freikorps Danmark', displaying the Danish flag and only in use for a short period in 1941.**

(Lower right) **Pair for an officer of the Hungarian 25.Waffen-Gren-Div der SS 'Hunyadi'.**

(Opposite below, bottom right patch) Blank officers' left patches are occasionally seen in foreign volunteer formations. This is probably due to the fact that officers of divisions termed 'Waffen-Grenadier ...' or 'Waffen-Gebirgs ... der SS' had the authority of their nominal ranks only within their own units. Their rank titles were e.g. 'Waffen-Untersturmführer' or 'Legions-Untersturmführer' rather than SS-Untersturmführer.

Collar patches

A selection of some foreign volunteer units' distinctive collar patches. Some were in general use; others were only rarely seen, with the SS-runes being worn in contravention of regulations. Some designs were worn by more than one unit as they were re-organised progressively during the war years.
(Top row, left to right) 23.SS-Freiw-Pz-Gren-Div 'Nederland'; 11.SS-Freiw-Pz-Gren-Div 'Nordland'; 18.SS-Pz-Gren-Div 'Horst Wessel'.
(Middle row) 25.W-Gren-Div der SS 'Hunyadi'; unidentified, possibly 24.W-Gebirgs (Karstjäger) Div der SS; 13.W-Gebirgs-Div der SS 'Handschar'.
(Bottom row) 20.W-Gren-Div der SS (estniche Nr.1); 30.W-Gren-Div der SS (weissruthenische Nr.1); 5.SS-Pz-Div 'Wiking' (never issued or worn).

(Top row, left to right) 21.W-Gebirgs-Div der SS 'Skanderbeg'; 15.W-Gren-Div der SS (lettische Nr.1). *(Middle row)* '36.W-Gren-Div der SS' (Regiment Dirlewanger); non-Germanic KL guards - also briefly worn by 19.W-Gren-Div der SS (lettische Nr.2). *(Bottom)* 27.SS-Freiw-Gren-Div 'Langemark'.

In the Waffen-SS, as throughout the Wehrmacht, shoulder straps displayed the wearer's rank and branch of service at a glance, and W-SS straps closely followed Army designs with only minor differences. Apart from general officers, all W-SS officers' straps have a black base upon which is a secondary layer of underlay in appropriate Waffenfarbe branch colour; the appropriate bullion braid or cord is then fixed on top, with or without 20mm gilt metal 'pips' (for officers below general rank).

The straps of W-SS NCOs differed from Army patterns mainly in that the upper side of the wool base of the strap was always in black. The same system of 9mm Tresse braid and white metal 'pips' denoted rank, with the outer piping in Waffenfarbe. The Tresse was made in bright metallic silver-

Officers' straps; each is shown twice, the upper side first followed by the underside.

(Left to right) SS-Sturmbannführer of Panzer troops; SS-Obersturmbannführer of infantry; SS-Brigadeführer.

NCOs' straps.
(Left to right)
SS-Scharführer of artillery; SS-Oberscharführer of Panzer troops, with cypher for divisional headquarters, officer quality in gilt metal; SS-Unterscharführer of cavalry.

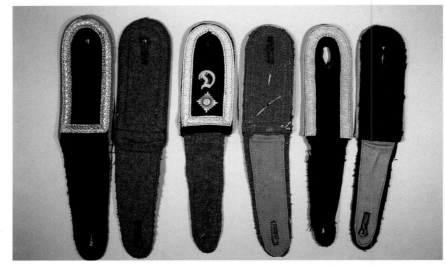

Enlisted ranks' straps.
(Left to right) Infantry, late war with rayon piping and 'SS-BW' stamp; infantry, wool piping and rayon tongue lining; cavalry, wool piping and cotton drill tongue lining.

coloured thread before the war; it later became available in a dull white brushed cotton, and the final version was in a subdued grey for combat wear. In practice all three types might be seen on combat uniforms throughout the war. Enlisted mens' straps were also all black, piped round the outside with the wearer's Waffenfarbe. Some manufacturers finished the underside of NCO and enlisted straps in black, but most used field-grey wool. Two types of attachment tongue are encountered: one tapers from the width of the strap's base to a point, and the other narrows inward immediately and thereafter is cut to the same width along its full length. Various reinforcing materials were also used on the back of the tongue, usually scraps left over from the lining of tunics.

Officers' straps. *(Left to right)* SS-Obersturmführer of cavalry; SS-Untersturmführer of mountain troops; SS-Obersturmbannführer of signals troops.

NCOs' straps. *(Left to right)* SS-Unterscharführer of mountain rifles; SS-Scharführer of Panzer troops, with 'Leibstandarte Adolf Hitler' slip-on cypher; SS-Scharführer of signals troops.

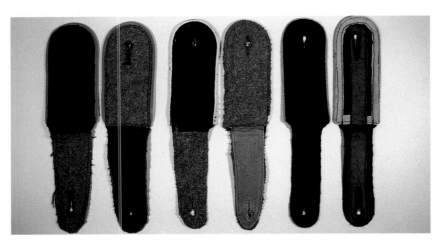

Enlisted ranks' straps. *(Left to right)* Artillery, with wool piping and black cotton tongue lining; infantry, with wool piping and grey cotton tongue lining; mountain rifles - here a very light shade of green used on a final production strap. Note also the lack of lining to the underside, and the narrow tongue.

In the Waffen-SS various shoulder strap devices were used to denote élite regiments and specialist units. Stamped metal cyphers were worn by senior NCOs in a silver finish and by officers in a gilt finish; stitched cyphers on removable slip-on cloth loops were displayed by junior enlisted ranks. A few of the better known cyphers are illustrated here.

(Above: left to right, top to bottom) Shoulder strap for a Panzertruppe SS-Obersturmführer in the 'Leibstandarte Adolf Hitler', with a heavily worn gilt 'LAH' cypher. Shoulder strap for an artillery SS-Oberscharführer with what appears to be a gilt officer's cypher of the 'Der Führer' Regiment in the 'Das Reich' Division. Slip-on enlisted grade cypher for the 'LAH', as introduced in mid-1940 to replace the cypher embroidered directly into the top of the shoulder strap. Front and back of stamped metal 'LAH' cyphers for senior NCO ranks. Note the fine gauge of metal used in the stamping, and the double prongs soldered to the rear. Front and back of officer's gilt metal cypher for the 'Germania' Regiment of the 'Das Reich' Division. Slip-on cypher for the 'Nordland' Regiment, also worn for a short period in 1943 by members of the division of that name. Several other regiments also used similar single-letter cyphers.

(Right) Enlarged front and back detail of stamped officers' cyphers for the 'Der Führer' Regiment, left, and the 'Leibstandarte Adolf Hitler', right. They are stamped from fine gauge aluminium with a gilt finish; each has two flat sheet fixing prongs.

(Left) SS-Oberscharführer of the 'Der Führer' Regiment wearing the field-grey special uniform for assault artillery crews. Apart from insignia of rank, branch and regiment he also displays (see also page 84) the Iron Cross 1st Class, the General Assault Badge, and the ribbon of the Iron Cross 2nd Class over that of the Winter 1941/42 Eastern Front medal.

(Right) SS-Oberscharführer of the 'Das Reich' Division wearing the M1942 helmet and M1936 service tunic; his sleeve eagle is BeVo-made, of NCO quality. His awards are the Infantry Assault Badge, the black Wound Badge, and the ribbon of the War Merit Medal.

Because the SS was originally a political organisation rather than a branch of the armed services (Wehrmacht), none of its evolving armed units - the SS-Verfügungstruppe, the Totenkopfverbände, and eventually the Waffen-SS - was entitled to wear the national eagle on the right breast. Instead the SS designed their own form of national eagle to be worn on the upper left sleeve of the service uniform. The first pattern introduced in 1936 (see page 67) had slightly 'wavy' outstretched wings, and the head faced to the left as viewed. This was replaced in 1938 by the definitive

Enlisted grade eagles.
(Top to bottom, left)
Machine-embroidered in white; machine-embroidered in white; machine-woven BeVo in white.
(Top to bottom, centre)
Machine-embroidered in grey; machine-embroidered foreign-made example, possibly Finnish; screen-printed final manufacture.
(Right) Two examples of machine-woven BeVo in tropical tan.

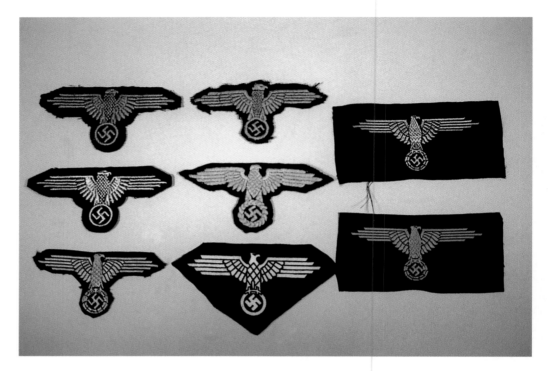

Officer grade eagles were of the same design, but manufactured to give a silver finish, usually in aluminium bullion thread. Shown here are two sleeve eagles and one smaller example for use on the field cap (sidecap).

(Opposite) The insignia on the enlisted ranks' field cap (sidecap) consisted of a BeVo national eagle above a death's-head, machine-woven in either off-white or light grey thread on a black backing. Officers had the same badges but in silver bullion. When the Model 1943 Einheitsfeldmütze was introduced the skull was retained at the front of the cap and the eagle was worn on the left side of the

flap above the ear. Later the two were both worn on the front of the cap. Finally, in 1944 the two were combined into a single-piece badge on a trapezoid shaped backing; the insignia were in a pearl-grey colour on green backing (or on black for Panzer caps). These insignia were available in a machine-woven pattern from BeVo of Wuppertal, and also in machine-embroidered cotton on wool. There was

apparently no officer's version of this combined badge.

(Left top) Cap eagle in pearl-white BeVo weave; the brown tone is discoloration from use.

(Left bottom) BeVo death's-head for the field cap in tropical tan thread; an identical design in pearl-grey was worn on field-grey caps. Note the manufacturer's marking which

appears at the cutting line of each piece.

(Right) BeVo machine-woven combined badge on black for the Panzer M1943 field cap. Note the dotted line marking the cutting point; all these types of pieces were woven on a continuous roll of base material and then cut into individual pieces. The badge for the field-grey cap is identical but with a green base colour.

design, which was worn until the end of the war; its head faced to the right as viewed, and the wingtips were more stylised. Initially it was manufactured in white (later grey) machine embroidery on black wool, and this is the most commonly encountered version. It was later replaced by a variant in

machine-woven cotton by BeVo of Wuppertal. This pattern also appeared in a sand colour for wear on tropical uniform. Finally, a crude screen-printed version was produced, but probably not issued before the end of the war.

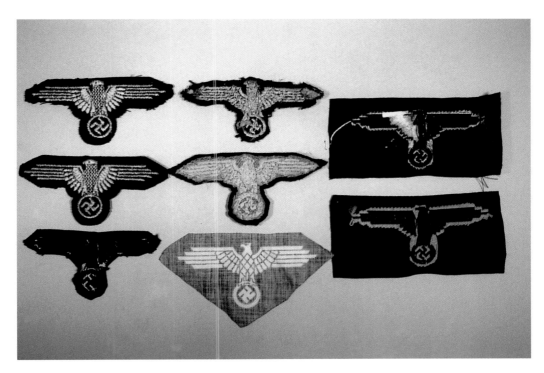

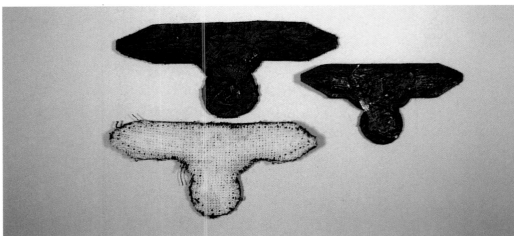

(Left) Among all kinds of hand-embroidered insignia variations may be encountered due to differing techniques and manufacturers. Often highlights were picked out in cotton thread to define the design. The back was usually sealed with paper to prevent thread-pulling. Officers' eagles for both tunic and field cap were later available in a fine silver cotton BeVo machine-woven form.

Foreign volunteer arm shields

Foreign volunteers served in large numbers in the Waffen-SS. They were usually grouped into ethnically based units, but often several of these units were assigned to a single division, making identification of different personnel difficult. Some of the collar patch designs used by foreign units were rather obscure and not immediately helpful. The use of national sleeve badges identified a soldier's nationality at a glance. They also echoed Himmler's favoured propaganda image of the Waffen-SS as a truly international 'European army' united against Bolshevism.

(Left to right, top row) **French, RZM pattern with black border; French, variant with horizontal stripes; French, machine-embroidered variant, also made in BeVo; Croatian, RZM pattern with black border.**

(Middle row) **Walloon (Belgium), SS pattern in limited use; Flemish (Belgium), RZM pattern; Flemish, early indigenous 'Legion Flandern' pattern; Italy, RZM pattern, possibly never worn.**

(Bottom row) **Holland, RZM pattern; Norway, RZM pattern; Norway, indigenous early pattern; Finland, later RZM pattern shield replacing indigenous patterns.**

(Top row, left to right) **Latvia, locally made shield for police units later used by SS troops; Latvia, machine-woven shield produced for the SS only; Latvia, first pattern, locally produced without title; Latvia, final RZM pattern with black border.**

(Bottom row) **Estonia, RZM pattern; Estonia, German-manufactured variant; Galicia (Ukraine), BeVo shield worn prior to November 1944; Albania, RZM pattern.**

Such badges usually took the form of the country's national flag or some other relevant national or ethnic emblem. Many were initially made indigenously in the various countries where volunteer units were raised, but later production was standardised by the RZM. The shields were usually worn on the left upper or lower sleeve, but many variations are encountered, especially with eastern troops, who often wore the shield on the right sleeve contrary to regulations. The selection of badges shown here are a representative sample only. The reverse of the examples shown are also illustrated for comparison.

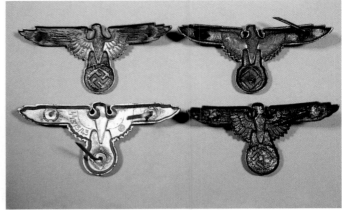

(Above & top) **The metal service cap insignia introduced for the SS in 1934 consisted of the SS pattern national eagle, and the death's-head which was the organisation's specific badge. (The Totenkopf had a long history in German military symbolism, stretching from élite Prussian hussar regiments of the 18th century, through the 'Black Brunswickers' of the Napoleonic Wars, to the Freikorps volunteer units of the German civil and border wars of 1918-22.) The design of these badges remained unchanged until the end of the war, and they were worn on both officers' and enlisted ranks' caps.**

Originally the badges were stamped in German silver, later in brass with a silver wash, steel, aluminium, and finally in zinc which was polished or painted. The mountings were either round pins or flat sheet prongs, and were soldered on to the back of the badge, often on a small circular mounting platform stamped as part of the badge's reverse side. The insignia were also stamped with the RZM logo and the maker's RZM number, this being the official sanction of production. Designs varied little from maker to maker, but slight variations will be encountered.

(Opposite) **One of the most distinctive items of insignia worn by Waffen-SS troops was the cuff title. This band of embroidered cloth was to become a symbol for many units and formations, and a source of great pride; it held the same place in a soldier's regard as a British regiment's cap badge or an American divisional shoulder patch. The Wehrmacht in general and the Waffen-SS in particular understood the morale value of specialist badges and élite distinctions; for this reason cuff titles were even awarded to some foreign volunteer units.**

Several patterns of manufacture are encountered, and may be grouped generally as follows: machine-embroidered by the RZM; hand-embroidered; machine-woven (usually referred to as 'BeVo').

Cuff titles will not be covered in great detail here; notes will be found on the pages devoted to relevant uniforms throughout this book, and several fine publications are available which specifically discuss the details of the many patterns and examples made. Illustrated opposite are several examples of the three basic techniques of manufacture mentioned above.

(Left) The reverse of cuff titles can reveal a good deal more about their construction and originality than the front. Note how the machine-embroidered 'Deutschland' officer's title (top) has a hand-sewn cotton backing panel over the letters to prevent unravelling of the wire thread. Lower down, the two officers' hand-embroidered cuff titles (third & fourth) show the remnants of the paper backing which was glued in place for the same purpose. The machine-woven title from BeVo of Wuppertal (bottom) shows the loose vertical threads that surround the lettering; and the very fine line of dots behind the white borders. The presence of these small dots is one sign of an original BeVo-manufactured piece; copies tend to have a much thicker design with dots and vertical dashes.

(Right, top to bottom) 'Deutschland' Regiment, machine-embroidered flat wire for officers. 'Deutschland' Regiment, machine-embroidered RZM pattern for enlisted ranks. 'Norge' Regiment, hand-embroidered for officers. 'Thule' Regiment, hand-embroidered for officers. 'Der Führer' Regiment, machine-woven BeVo pattern for enlisted ranks. 'Reichführer-SS' Division, machine-woven BeVo pattern for enlisted ranks.

MISCELLANEA

(*Left*) The badge for qualified mountain guides in the Waffen-SS Gebirstruppe was introduced in late 1944. It was in the form of an oval patch with an Edelweiss flower and the legend 'Bergführer' ('mountain leader'), and was worn on the left chest pocket of the tunic. Shown here are the officer grade version in hand-embroidered bullion, and the machine-embroidered enlisted ranks' pattern. The officer's badge is still mounted on a tunic pocket, and was obtained from a museum in St.Petersburg (Leningrad), Russia.

(*Right*) Four examples of the paper RZM labels introduced in the late 1930s for SS cloth insignia, and mostly found on Waffen-SS items. The large letter on the upper left identifies the level of work undertaken, 'A' being the most basic and 'F' being the most difficult. The number on the upper right is the manufacturer's identity code number. The number and letter at the bottom indicate the item number, which is sequential for each piece manufactured. Due to the sheer numbers of items being made during the war, the work was contracted out and the label system was discontinued around the beginning of 1943.

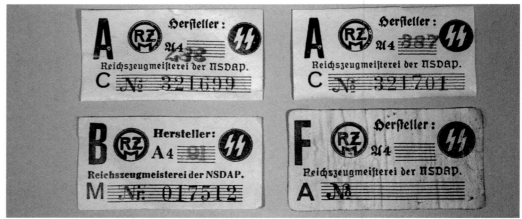

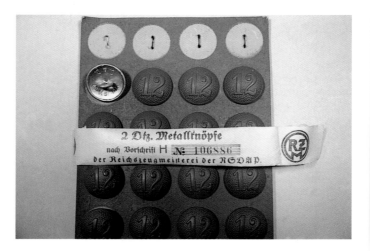

(*Left*) A sheet of numbered buttons manufactured in the pre-war period by the RZM. It is interesting to note that the buttons have been painted while already mounted on the card; and that the rear carries the RZM logo and the manufacturer's code.

The belt and buckle for Waffen-SS officers was simply a continuation of that worn in the Allgemeine-SS. The design remained unchanged from around 1933 until 1945. The buckle was usually 45mm in size and was worn with a black leather belt for service wear and a brocade belt for full dress. In the pre- and early war period the belt was also worn with a cross strap which passed over the right shoulder. During the war most officers wore the simple Wehrmacht pattern brown leather officer's belt with a plain two-pronged, pebble finished white metal frame buckle. The ornate SS belt with its simple hook closure was too easily opened for safe wear with field equipment.

Illustrated on these pages are four examples of enlisted grade belt buckles. The design of the buckle remained unchanged throughout the period of the Third Reich: a national eagle of composite shape, owing something to the first 'wavy-winged' style but facing right as viewed, and the SS motto *'Meine Ehre heißt Treue!'* ('My honour is loyalty'). They were produced in steel and in aluminium, with several different retaining clasps depending on the manufacturer. Some early retainers were moulded as part of the buckle, while later examples had the catch welded or brazed onto the plate.

(Left) Three examples of issue-stamped enlisted belt leathers. These were generally 45mm wide. All incorporate the RZM logo, the last number in the serial being the date of issue. The belt at the bottom is unissued and was one of a batch found in Norway several years ago.

Early buckles were in a dull silver finish, while wartime buckles were painted either field-grey or, late in the war, a dark blue-grey. Virtually all buckles were RZM and maker code marked; however, late-war examples may be marked only with the maker's logo (such as the blue-grey 'RODO'-marked example, shown as the lower of this pair), or may bear no markings at all. Note also that like the belt stampings, the number after the forward slash (e.g. '40' on the upper of these two buckles) is the year of manufacture.

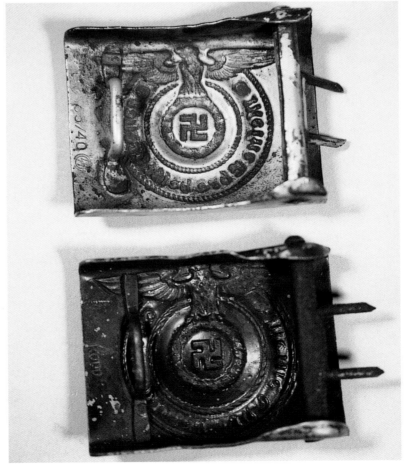

Every soldier in the Wehrmacht, including the Waffen-SS, wore around his neck an Erkennungsmarke or identification tag. The tag was oval, 7cm at its widest, and made of either aluminium or zinc sheet metal. Across the centre were three perforations, allowing the tab to be broken in two in the case of the owner's death; one piece remained around the neck of the deceased and the other was turned in to the unit's headquarters for registration.

The tags were stamped with the units title (always abbreviated); the wearer's number on the unit roll (Stammrollnummer); and his blood group. There are some rare examples of impressed Waffen-SS Totenkopf unit tags, but almost all are stamped with a punch set. Tags without blood groups may be found, these being unused tags from unit stocks. Illustrated (right) are some examples of tags recovered from the site of a former prisoner of war camp in Latvia.

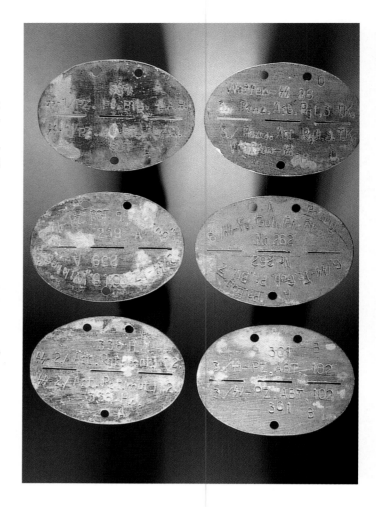

(Left to right, top row) **SS-1/PZ.PI.BTL. LAH** (1st Company, Armoured Pioneer Battalion 'Leibstandarte Adolf Hitler'); **Waffen-SS 3./Panz. Art. Rgt 3.T.K** (3rd Company, Armoured Artillery Regiment 3 'Totenkopf').

(Middle) **2./SS-PZ.RGT.5 "WIKING"** (2nd Company, Tank Regiment 5 'Wiking'); **6./SS.Fr.Geb. Pi.Btl.7 Pr.Eug.** (6th Company, Volunteer Mountain Pioneer Battalion 7 'Prinz Eugen').

(Bottom) **SS-2/Art.Rgt. (mot).12 H.J.** (2nd Company, Motorised Artillery Regiment 12 'Hitlerjugend'); **3./SS-PZ.ABT.102** (3rd Company, Tank Detachment 102).

(Below) **An identity tag for Stab/SS Pz.Gr.Rgt. Nordland** (Staff Company, Armoured Grenadier Regiment 'Nordland') as it was recovered, in a small leather pouch. Many soldiers privately purchased these from the unit canteen to hold their tag and prevent chafing.

(Opposite top) **The awards belonging to SS-Sturmbannführer Alfred Arnold** - see note on page 22.

(Left to right, top row) **Deutsches Kreuz in case** - awarded posthumously, 6 January 1944; two separate ribbon bars, including a miniature for the SS Long Service medal; Iron Cross 1st Class; Infantry Assault Badge; Winter 1941/42 Eastern Front medal; War Merit Cross 2nd Class with Swords.

(Bottom) **Bronze DRL sports badge; Bronze SA sports badge; Bronze Rider's Award badge; Wound Badge in black** (first & second wounds); **Wound Badge in silver** (third & fourth wounds).

(Opposite bottom) **Arnold's first Wound Badge in its original issue packet, with the award document.** He was wounded 'near Charkow' (Kharkov) on 19 February 1943, as a captain in SS Regiment 'Thule' with the 'Totenkopf' Division - at that date designated a Kradschützen-Regiment (motorcycle regiment). The document is signed by a senior medical officer.

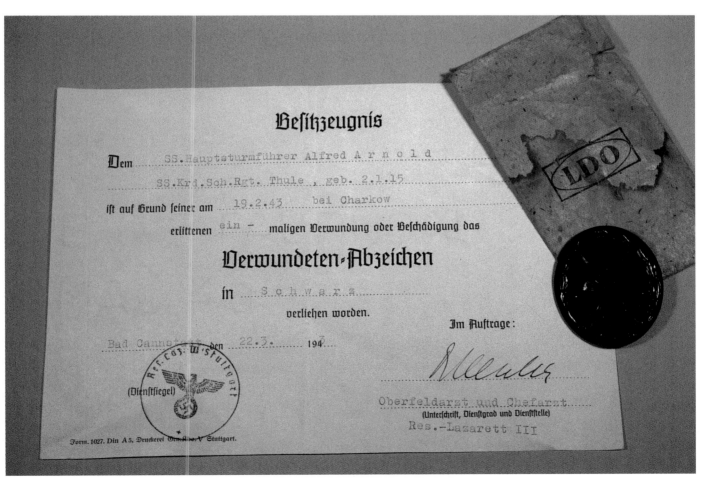

Waffen-SS soldiers carried an identification book which contained all their relevant details such as pay, issue of uniforms and equipment, awards, etc. This was termed the Soldbuch ('paybook'). Two patterns of this document will be encountered for Waffen-SS soldiers: one has the standard Wehrmacht brown cover, and the other a light grey cover showing the title 'SS Soldbuch'. There seems to have been no particular reason for a soldier being issued one or the other pattern, and this was presumably simply a question of availability of the specifically SS version, which is less often seen.

A Soldbuch of the standard Wehrmacht pattern, issued to SS-Sturmann Fritz Lederer. He served first in the Panzer-Grenadier Replacement Battalion 'Germania' and was then posted to the 7th Company of Panzer Regiment 1 'Leibstandarte SS Adolf Hitler'. His identity photogaph is interesting, showing him wearing the black Panzer service tunic with 'LAH' slip-on shoulder strap cyphers, and a field-grey SS sidecap without insignia attached; the reason for this is not known. Note also that the first page gives details of the wearer's Erkennungsmarke (identity tag). The Soldbuch, being a personal document, can answer many questions about a soldier and give a fascinating insight into his service.

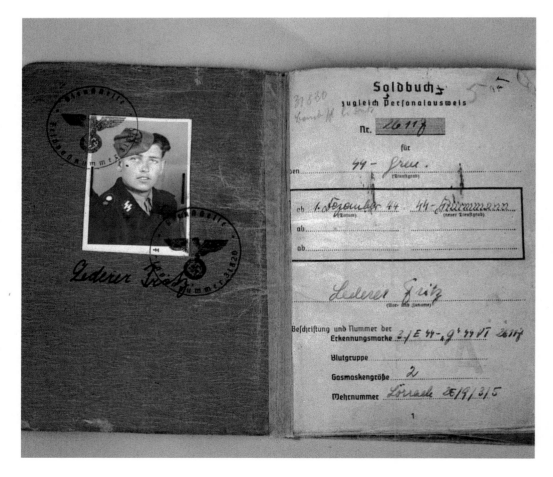

Two photographs of the SS pattern Soldbuch for SS-Mann Freidrich Paijonseck (?). He was inducted into the Panzer-Grenadier Replacement & Training Battalion (Ausbildung und Ersatz Bataillon) of the 'Leibstandarte SS Adolf Hitler', and immediately transferred with the training cadre to build and train the fledgling 'Hitlerjugend' Division at Beverloo in Belgium. In his identity photograph he wears the slip-on cyphers of the 'LAH'. Note the stamp at the top of the first page, giving his rank as 'SS-Pz-Gren.' (SS Panzer-Grenadier); and the round unit stamp on the second page for SS-Pz-Gren-Ers-Btl. 'LSSAH'.

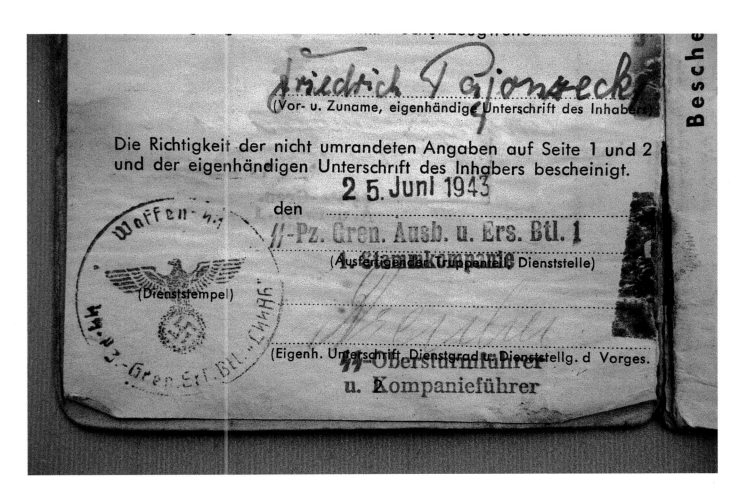

SELECT BIBLIOGRAPHY

Angolia, John, *Cloth Insignia of the SS*, R.James Bender
Publishing Co., San Jose CA, USA (1983)

Angolia, John, *Belt Buckles & Brocades*, R.James Bender
Publishing Co., San Jose CA, USA (1982)

Beaver, Michael D., & Borsarello, J.F., *Camouflage Uniforms of
the Waffen-SS*, Schiffer Publishing Ltd., Atglen PA, USA
(1995)

Buss, Philip Henry, & Mollo, Andrew, *Hitler's Germanic
Legions*, Macdonald & Jane's Ltd., London, UK (1978)

Hicks, Kelly, *SS Helmets: A Collector's Guide*, Reddick
Enterprises, Denison TX, USA (1993)

Lumsden, Robin, *SS Regalia*, Bison Books Ltd., London, UK
(1995)

Mollo, Andrew, *Uniforms of the SS*, 6 vols, Windrow & Greene
Ltd, London, UK (1997)

Ulric of England, *SS and Political Cuffbands*, Ulric Publishing,
Surrey, UK (1998)

Wikberg, Olli, *Meine Ehre heißt Treue!*, Wiking-Divisioona Oy,
Helsinki, Finland (1999)

Windrow, Martin, *The Waffen-SS, MAA 34* (Revised Edn.),
Osprey Publishing Ltd., London, UK (1982)